COMMENTS ON *MENSURAM BONAM*

"*Mensuram Bonam* is a timely and most helpful document calling for necessary re-adjustments and value-shifts of our financial system. It convincingly raises the investor's focus from mere sustainability to true stewardship based on Catholic Social Teaching and responsible faith-consistent investing. It reminds investors explicitly that their decisions have to be compliant with the core mission of their institutions and directed towards the fulfilment of this mission."
Cardinal Christoph Schönborn, Archbishop of Vienna

"In an increasingly uncertain world, entrepreneurs and investors alike need a beacon to make investment decisions. It is of course a question of studying the risk and the profitability of the opportunity, but today we must go further, by also evaluating the social and environmental impact of this decision. It is an ethical imperative, informed by the social teaching of the Church. For all those of good will who are ready to take up this challenge, this publication is essential."
Bruno Bobone, President, UNIAPAC, the Christian Entrepreneurs Confederation

"Deep congratulations for another very rich and useful document."
Pierre Lecocq (UNIAPAC)

"I welcome the publication of *Mensuram Bonam*. It is a vital intervention into a financial system that fails to serve the common good by focusing on the 'here and now' rather than the interests of long-term human flourishing. It should be essential reading for all investors."
Reverend Canon Edward Carter, Chair of the Church Investors Group

"We warmly commend you for the timely release of *Mensuram Bonam*, as it is completely consistent with the work of the Global Foundation, in encouraging investors and finance more generally to serve a sustainable, global common good. This initiative should be welcomed and supported by all of those from the private sector and communities worldwide who wish to act with greater purpose in their professional lives."

Steve Howard, The Global Foundation

"The UK's Impact Investing Institute welcomes the Catholic Church's active engagement with the world of finance and investment, and its call in *Mensuram Bonam* to its institutions to commit to faith-consistent investing that is entirely compatible with modern, progressive thinking on impact and sustainable investing."

Sarah Gordon, CEO and James Broderick, Deputy Chair, Impact Investing Institute

"The journey toward a sustainable future has started. It is a journey deeply connected to our duty as human beings on this planet and as Christian brothers and sisters with creation. All the more if we are entrusted with the responsibility of managing money and making investments, we have to be professional and prophetic. We have to make an impact and change the system not just simply commit to best efforts. With the Christian Social Thought we have a goal. With *Fratelli Tutti* and *Laudato Si'* we have a compass. With *Mensuram Bonam* we have a roadmap. The journey goes on."

Bertrand Badré, Managing Partner and Founder, Blue like an Orange Sustainable Capital

MENSURAM BONAM

Faith-Based Measures for Catholic Investors

A Starting Point and Call to Action

The Pontifical Academy
of Social Sciences

EDITED BY
Cardinal Peter Turkson,
Jean-Baptiste de Franssu, and John Dalla Costa

Paulist Press
New York / Mahwah, NJ

Scripture quotations are based on the New Revised Standard Version Bible: Catholic Edition, copyright © 1989, 1993 National Council of the Churches of Christ in the United States of America. Used by permission. All rights reserved worldwide.

Cover images by AKalenskyi/Shutterstock.com (scales); vachira thongkhuanluek/Shutterstock.com (bar graph); totiart/Shutterstock.com (dove); and gomolach/Shutterstock.com (wheat)
Cover and book design by Lynn Else

Copyright © 2022 by the Pontifical Academy of Social Sciences

All rights reserved. No part of this publication may be reproduced, stored in a retrieval system, or transmitted in any form or by any means, electronic, mechanical, photocopying, recording, scanning, or otherwise, without either the prior written permission of the Publisher, or authorization through payment of the appropriate per-copy fee to the Copyright Clearance Center, Inc., www.copyright.com. Requests to the Publisher for permission should be addressed to the Permissions Department, Paulist Press, permissions@paulistpress.com.

Library of Congress Cataloging-in-Publication Data available upon request.

ISBN 978-0-8091-5826-3 (paperback)
ISBN 978-0-8091-8977-9 (ebook)

Published by Paulist Press
997 Macarthur Boulevard
Mahwah, New Jersey 07430
www.paulistpress.com

Printed and bound in the
United States of America

CONTENTS

Foreword *by Roger Aguinaldo* vii

Foreword *by Cardinal Peter Turkson* ix

Introduction..xiii

   What investors need and what is needed from investors. xiii

   Human development from the values of faith. xiv

   Good measures. Only a beginning. xv

   Who is MB for?..xvii

Chapter I: The Principles for *Mensuram Bonam* 1

   Guidance from faith and Catholic Social Teaching. 1

   Pillars of faith: Investing in the Catholic key. 5

      God's self-revelation as the basis of faith, and for co-commitment to the common good. 6

      Call to enquiry and examen. 6

      Fidelity to God's covenant through Jesus Christ. 6

      Call to vocation. 7

      Participating in the love and wonder of the Trinity. 8

      Call "to read reality in a Trinitarian key." 8

      In the embrace of grace. 9

      Call to discernment. 10

      Shaped by the Word of God. 11

      Call for "lectio divina." 11

CONTENTS

With the Holy Spirit. *"Abide in my love."* 12
Catholic Social Teaching (CST): Good measures for investor guidance and practice. 13
   Call to re-set vision and responsibilities. 22
   Call to develop and deepen best-responsibility practices. 23
   Call to imagine what is needed—and what is possible—for integral human development. 23

Chapter II. The Practical Guidance from *Mensuram Bonam* 29

  Getting started. Adopting a faith-based process. 31
  Lessons from Catholic innovators. 34
  Faith-consistent investing (FCI) in practice. 38
    Call to engage. 38
    Call to enhance. 40
    Call to exclude. 47
  Habits for practicum. 49

Conclusion 55
  Sharing the work. 55
  Only a beginning. What's next? 57

Appendix—Exclusionary Criteria 59

Notes 63

Bibliography 71

FOREWORD

As I reflect on my 35+ years in the secular asset and investment management industry, I am reminded of the countless lessons learned and invaluable experiences gained throughout my career. I have witnessed the transformative power of strategic investments and the profound impact they can have on individuals, communities, and the world at large. Yet it is only in recent years that I have come to deeply appreciate the immense potential of aligning capital with faith-based principles.

This book is the result of a shared vision—a collaboration among many sponsors, each dedicated to empowering Catholic and Christian investors to steward resources with integrity and impact. As lead sponsors and supportive partners, we have come together to shape an international movement where conviction meets capital, and where financial excellence can coexist harmoniously with faith.

Rather than simply excluding what is misaligned, our collective mission is to champion investment strategies that are purpose-driven and ethically grounded. From responsible investment statements to faith-based public and alternative, permanent funds, each sponsor brings unique expertise and deep relationships—across dioceses, religious congregations, foundations, institutions, and family offices—helping to ensure that our efforts reflect the diversity and richness

> "More than a set of guidelines, *Mensuram Bonam* is a call to action for all Catholic investors to engage in practices that promote the common good."
>
> Roger Aguinaldo
> Founder Catholic Faith Investor Summit
> Managing Partner, Pray Investment Management

of our faith communities, and the over $2 trillion of institutional capital we represent.

For this inaugural Catholic Faith Investor Summit, we proudly present *Mensuram Bonam*, a guide for Catholic investors grounded in faith-based principles and Catholic Social Teaching. More than a set of guidelines, it is a call to action for ethical, responsible investing that promotes the common good. This book and Summit provide practical advice from Catholic innovators, offering a roadmap for implementing faith-driven investment strategies and ensuring financial activities reflect Catholic values.

United as sponsors and contributors, we believe there is a better way to invest—one that honors faith, delivers returns, and builds lasting legacy. Our commitment is to guide Catholic and Christian investors through financial complexities while remaining true to his Word. By embracing the principles of *Mensuram Bonam*, we can steward resources and make meaningful impact, demonstrating that faith and finance can work together to deliver our Catholic mission.

God Bless,

Roger Aguinaldo
Chairman, Catholic Faith Investor Summit
Co-Founder, Managing Partner, Pray Investment Management LLC
raguinaldo@prayim.com
+1-718-997-0799
https://www.linkedin.com/in/rogeraguinaldo

Thank you to the sponsors and supporters of the Inaugural Catholic Faith Investor Summit (as of this printing): Pray Investment Management, First Trust Global Portfolios, Beacon Pointe, Knights of Columbus Asset Advisors, Faith Investor Services, Arimathea, CapTrust, and Young Catholic Professionals.

FOREWORD

The Council Fathers, at the second session of the Second Vatican Council (1962-65), gave the Church a mandate to engage with the entire human family, with whom she is connected, in conversation and dialogue about its various problems. They believed this gesture would bear "witness to the faith of the Church and [be] an eloquent witness and proof of her solidarity with and respect for the human race."[1] Since then, several initiatives of the Dicasteries of the Roman Curia have sought to implement the Council's mandate. *Mensuram Bonam* (MB), the work that is presented here, is part of this tradition of Church initiatives seeking to engage in dialogue with the human family about its various experiences and challenges. With its publication, *Mensuram Bonam* hopes to shed the light of the Gospel and of Catholic Social Teaching (CST) on the specific area of economics and the world of finance which may be referred to as the management of financial assets or investing.

As agents of institutions and as individuals, people may be entrusted with assets to be invested, rather than merely spent. Since finance has taken on a larger role at every level of human activity, the need for the Church to reflect on the requirements of Christian discipleship, including the vocation of persons to stewardship in this arena, has become more critical. It is important that their stewardship of created goods, including all forms of financial activity, especially *asset management*, be directed to reflect this gift of God to the human family, by serving the common good, respecting justice and ethical standards.[2]

How the Church equips her faithful for such an exercise, calls to mind the observation of Pope Benedict XVI about the Church and Politics. Echoing the teaching of Vatican Council II, Pope Benedict XVI observes that *"the Church does not have technical solutions to offer,"*[3] and does not, therefore, interfere in any way in the politics of States. However, the Church does *"have a mission of truth to accomplish, in every time and circumstance, for a society that is attuned to man, to his dignity, to his vocation. [...] Fidelity to man requires fidelity to the truth, which alone is the guarantee of freedom (cf. Jn. 8:32) and of the possibility of integral human development."*[4] Mensuram Bonam adopts the same posture towards the world of finance. Accordingly, the light of the Gospel and of Catholic Social Teaching which MB seeks to shed on "the management of financial assets" belongs to the Church's *mission of truth*, which is not only the truth of *faith*, but also the truth of *reason*. The Church's social teaching is a particular application of this encounter between the *light of faith* and the *light of reason*.[5]

This call contained in MB could not come at a better time. As Pope Francis often observes, the ongoing crisis due to the Covid-19 pandemic has uncovered other pandemics of dysfunctional social systems, such as job insecurity, poor access to healthcare, food insecurity and corruption. But Pope Francis also sees this crisis as an opportunity to look at the future which we can dream about together and to discover *values* and *priorities* in the teaching of our faith and its wisdom for building such a future and inspiring our investing with faith-consistent criteria.

Rooted as it is in the teachings of faith and in the Church's social teaching, MB speaks to and supports all those, who work in the financial sectors every day (institutions but also individuals), and are searching for ways to live their faith and contribute to the promotion of an inclusive and integral well-being or advancement of people. MB seeks to offer such an opportunity for discernment, providing guidance and principles to enable them to

Foreword

respond to the call of the Gospel and the wisdom of the Tradition of the Church by more fully integrating the Church's social and moral teaching into the management of their financial assets with a focus on investing in listed securities or mutual funds.

The objective of this publication, is twofold:

i. where investment guidelines and criteria exist, entities should be encouraged to persevere in systematically integrating Catholic Social Teaching into their investment policies, and adjust them where necessary from time to time.
ii. where such guidelines have not yet been developed, MB is providing a stimulus and a model / example to help and to encourage institutions to establish clear investment policies by integrating Catholic Social Teaching into their investing process.

In building on the good work that has been accomplished by many in the Church as well as by our sisters and brothers in other faith traditions and men and women of good will, we hope that this Catholic Perspective on Faith-Consistent Investing will be a source of inspiration and guidance to Catholic institutions and believers and to willing listeners everywhere. For, drawn from the treasures of Church teaching, the proposals of this document look to the assistance of every person of our time, whether they believe in God, or do not explicitly recognize Him. If adopted, they will promote within the human family a sharper insight into its full destiny, and thereby lead it to fashion a world more to man's surpassing dignity, to search for a brotherhood which is universal and more deeply rooted, and to meet the urgencies of our age with a gallant and unified effort born of love[6] (cf. GS n.91).

Mensuram Bonam also looks forward in the coming years to following up on its engagement with the investment industry, to reflect on the principles that flow from their faith, value systems and mission in life.

We would now like to take this opportunity to thank heartily all who have contributed to the preparation of this *call to action*, as a dedicated working group,[7] engaged themselves in the *Church's mission of truth*, and *ECHo8 Fund* which facilitated the discussion of *Mensuram Bonam* in the Academy of Social Sciences of the Holy See.

Peter Kodwo Cardinal Turkson
*Chancellor: Pontifical Academies of
Sciences & of Social Sciences*
Vatican, 10.11.2022

> After pronouncing the Beatitudes in Luke's Gospel, and teaching love for enemies, Jesus says: "Do not judge, and you will not be judged; do not condemn, and you will not be condemned. Forgive, and you will be forgiven; give and it will be given to you. A good measure, pressed down, shaken together, running over, will be put in your lap. For the measure you give will be the measure you get back." (Luke 6:37-38)

INTRODUCTION

WHAT INVESTORS NEED AND WHAT IS NEEDED FROM INVESTORS.

1. Investing has never been as essential nor as demanding as now. Many uncertainties, including from geopolitical tensions, pandemics, and climate change, add dense ambiguities to even the most informed risk analyses. Further complicating decisions are the widening considerations for valuing financial returns within a nexus of social and ecological outcomes. Whether investors demand options that address these multiple responsibilities, or resist them, the very nature of investing is undergoing fundamental transformation. The volatility from our many global crises is unsettling markets and economic theories, placing investors in a precarious position. While managing from within the inherited economic paradigm—that is still in place, and still exerting powerful forces—investors must innovate the new criteria for assets and risks to create the economy being summoned for the future. Every investment is indispensable.

As well as create material capacities for the needed change, each and every investment gives tangible expression to values that either contribute to the future, or forsake it. Questions abound. Not only difficult questions, which stretch investors' capacities for evaluation to their limits, but also questions that defy answers; urgencies investors must begin to address even before new architectures of theory or norms are set.

2. This document—*Mensuram Bonam* (MB)—stands with investors in this crucible of quandaries and questions. Given what is at stake for humanity and future generations, MB makes a fervent 'call to action' for faith-based, faith-consistent, faith-inspired investing based on the light of the Gospel, and the guidance from Church teaching. Pope Francis stipulates that "purchasing is always a moral—and not simply an economic act."[9] Because of its power and potential, investing is especially fraught and freighted with these moral dimensions. Part of what makes this moment so confusing and threatening to investors is that prevailing economic theories have yet to take these dimensions into account. In the aftermath of the global financial crisis, Pope Benedict XVI corrected the notion that economics can function independently of ethics. He stressed that the validity and credibility of economic activity depended on ethics rooted in the potential of "integral human development."[10] What does this mean? Simply, that the true norm for progress, and for the economy, is the flourishing of humanness—what Saint Paul VI described, as the "transition from less than human conditions to truly human ones."[11]

HUMAN DEVELOPMENT FROM THE VALUES OF FAITH.

3. Inciting reflection among all investors on human values for development, MB specifically addresses Catholic investors

Introduction

with principles from faith from which to evaluate all their financial instruments. It must be acknowledged that many investors, including Catholics inspired by local Bishops Conferences, are already at work doing the exceedingly hard discerning of new patterns for responsible investment according to personal faith or values. Theirs have been among the trailblazing efforts that have realized today's exponential growth in ethical, green, socially responsible, or environmentally sustainable funds. MB celebrates these efforts and movements, and, at the same time, recognizes the momentum for structural change as more difficult for two basic reasons: motives and measures. For instance, are the aims and claims for responsible investment authentically rooted in integral human development? Or are human values being used instrumentally? Investors do have increasing options, however, at this point, these often only compound confusion because the purpose and credibility of innovations remain opaque, if not indecipherable. New measures are needed to set the norms for integral human development and to create trustworthy metrics for this multi-dimensional performance. MB draws on the wellspring of faith, using lessons from Scripture and Catholic Social Teaching to measurably grow investors' capacity for ethical reflection and moral innovation.

> MB draws on the wellspring of faith, using lessons from Scripture and Catholic Social Teaching to measurably grow investors' capacity for ethical reflection and moral innovation.

GOOD MEASURES. ONLY A BEGINNING.

4. *Mensuram Bonam* means *a good measure*. It continues the Church's engagement with the world of business and finance to exercise her *mission of truth* in light of the Gospel. As spoken

by Jesus in Luke's Gospel, the *good measure* has multiple implications. It refers to the personal and social surplus to be realized when human relations leaven existing norms of reciprocity with the mercy and forgiveness gifted by God. Such gifts from God's "superabundance" also set the ethical norm for faith—the moral measure to gauge how belief is lived.

Other implications await further reflection and study of this passage. For investors, and for this context, the good measure initiated by MB has twofold implications. One is to provide a preliminary process for formulating faith-based standards—the measures or steps to take to discern what faith beckons in the here-and-now. Navigating tensions between financial fiduciary duty and faith's duties for a just and sustainable common home, cannot be reduced to a checklist. Without presuming outcomes, MB sets out processes for reflection to further develop facility with using faith and reason; and for dialogue to learn from innovators and inspire collaboration.

The other meaning of good measure is to begin the immensely hard and long-term work of generating valid metrics for evaluating integral human development. Important frameworks have already been launched, such as for the United Nations Sustainable Development Goals (SDG). Trajectories for measuring just, inclusive and ecologically-sound practices are being fashioned by the UN and elsewhere. However, there is no investment algorithm for simulating human conscience. Even careful measures, using the most comprehensive data available, are limited by having to project future possibility from precedent. Under the aegis of the Pontifical Academy of Social Sciences (PASS), MB encourages the interdisciplinary work of scientists and scholars to better understand complexity and systems, which are crucial for investment metrics. Still, morals involve another order of calculus that numbers represent only imperfectly. MB serves the real economy, and its ethical moorings, by promoting the common good at the service of integral

Introduction

human development. In short, MB upholds the personhood of every human being as the central measure of social order, and to create "a narrative of human dignity that leaves no one behind."[12]

WHO IS MB FOR?

5. MB calls all Catholics involved in investing to formally adopt and apply faith-based criteria in the *stewardship of their finances*. Specifically, MB addresses both those investors now beginning this process of reconsideration, as well as those continuing to refine their investment horizon and practices. In the light of Vatican II, all work is regarded as the opportunity to enact discipleship in everyday life.[13] Saint Paul VI recognized "everyone who works as a creator." Underscoring this concept, Pope Benedict XVI writes that "Business activity has a human significance, prior to its professional one," meaning that "both professional competence and moral consistency are necessary."[14] For investors of faith, this means, as a starting point, giving due consideration to reconciling economic objectives with the overarching principles of the Church's moral and social teachings. It also enjoins Catholic investors to use their expertise, skills of engagement, and ethical concerns, to contribute to changing economic culture so as to accelerate the flourishing of integral human development.

6. The *Compendium of the Social Doctrine of the Church* has been the primary source for the principles for faith-consistent investing developed in MB. Numerous projects have already been launched to promote appreciation of the Church's social teaching in all human spheres. In service to the world of business and economics, symposia and publications have explored the vocational aspects of business leadership and education,[15] and addressed ethical foundations for renewing the economy after the global financial crisis.[16] More recently, Pope Francis

has invited professionals in audit, finance and strategy to form a new generation that he calls "integral consultants." The Holy Father explains that a great deal can be done to address the multiple crises afflicting our world by "organizing their analyses and proposals with an integral perspective and vision."[17] Extrapolating from Pope Francis' insight, MB supports a new generation of what could be called "integral investors," providing Church teachings to inspire vision and develop perspective that is wider and more inclusive.

7. MB specifically addresses Catholics—those overseeing the Church's assets and her investments and institutions, those responsible for Catholic organizations, institutions, and orders, as well as individual Catholics investors, Catholic educators, and students in business, finance and investment, among others. At the same time, MB recognizes that the faith-guidance for investors has rational resonance across many religious traditions. Honesty, trust, truth, justice, mercy, sincerity, responsibility, accountability, and the basic reciprocity of The Golden Rule are examples of widely shared virtues. Pope Francis reinforces the gifts of this collaboration as sisters and brothers: "The urgent challenge to protect our common home includes a concern to bring the whole human family together to seek a sustainable and integral development, for we know that things can change… Humanity still has the ability to work together in building our common home."[18]

Chapter I
THE PRINCIPLES FOR *MENSURAM BONAM*

GUIDANCE FROM FAITH AND CATHOLIC SOCIAL TEACHING

8. The ethics of "investing" for Catholics are already encoded in the word's etymology. In Latin, *investire* means "to dress, to clothe," and "to endow with authority." In the Bible, the first act of literal investing occurs in the book of Genesis, when God—having expelled Adam and Eve from the Garden of Eden for their disobedience—"made garments of skins for the man, and his wife, and clothed them" (Genesis 3:21). Adam and Eve had hid from God out of shame for their nakedness. By making these clothes for them, God in effect eased their fears and restored the capability for relationship. God's merciful act is future-looking and generative. It anticipates the vulnerability of Adam and Eve, and provides, in this gift of protection, the bodily and personal security for them to assume their agency in God's creation. So it remains today, with each investment trading-off risk (or vulnerability) for future protections and benefits. Investing can rightly be regarded as a vocation because it is a capability inherited from God to creatively foresee, mitigate, and resolve creaturely vulnerabilities. Assuming this vocation, and fostering its development, requires that investors complement their technical expertise with prayerful reflection. For investors with faith,

the view of the world formed by numbers and analytics is forever incomplete. Even brief moments in the presence of Scripture, or quick references to the Church's teachings, can fill-in by grace or wisdom those ethical gaps in perspective or process.

> For investors with faith, the view of the world formed by numbers and analytics is forever incomplete. Even brief moments in the presence of Scripture, or quick references to the Church's teachings, can fill-in by grace or wisdom those ethical gaps in perspective or process.

9. In the plan of God, women and men have been endowed with intellectual powers by which they may grow in wisdom so as to understand their collective responsibility to each other and to creation—all as part of an integral ecology. Relying on both faith and reason, and under the guidance of the Holy Spirit, persons may discern together the foundations and principles underpinning well-functioning systems, including finance and investments. In turn, these truths assist in forming operating processes and practices which are essential in guiding institutions and individuals as they participate in finance. In MB, the proposal of a *faith-consistent* investing guide is inspired primarily by the wisdom transmitted by the Catholic Church that is based on the Sacred Scriptures and the living Tradition in the Church, as interpreted by the Magisterium. Through the gift of faith, God's revelation broadens humanity's horizons and satisfies our deep longing for truth and the ultimate meaning of human life.

10. *Faith-based* is perhaps the original designation for this pivot to investing as an enactment of discipleship in Jesus Christ. Others today use a variety of terms such as faith-formed, faith-informed, faith-consistent, faith-aligned, and faith-inspired, among others. In practice, investors reflecting on their faith use a matrix of questions and prompts—probing the Scriptures,

enquiring of Church Teaching, summoning their own ethical wisdom, and striving in their own way for openness to the gifts of the Holy Spirit.

11. The concerns motivating MB have in fact been experienced on the ground, in real life. Numerous local and regional Episcopal Conferences have already undertaken social analysis in light of the Church's teaching. And from these local concerns, bishops have identified principles for change that apply to the faithful, including investors. By example, the Austrian Bishops' Conference observed that "wealth" supplies the "economic basis for institutions and people." It exerts a profound influence on the structure of a society. Accordingly, the Austrian Bishops conclude that "because you can do something with it [wealth], there is an obligation to use this ability responsibly."[19] Similarly, and echoing the teachings for integral human development, the US Bishops note that "Economic life raises important social and moral questions for each of us and for society as a whole. Like family life, economic life is one of the chief areas where we live out our faith, love our neighbor, confront temptation, fulfill God's creative design, and achieve our holiness."[20] Investing with faith is therefore a milieu for vocation. As well as personal conversion, CST aims to make the common sphere, including markets and culture, more humanizing. Towards this aim, the Italian Bishops' Conference reminds the faithful that "ethics belongs to finance as something of its own and that it arises from within itself. It is not added after, but emanates from an intimate need of finance itself to pursue its own goals, since the latter is also a human activity."[21]

Other Catholic and Church institutions (such as the IOR—*Istituto per le Opere di Religione*) have also developed norms for managing finances with conscience from the demands of faith. Significant progress has been made specifying accountabilities as well as engaging securities issuers for reform. Enhanced by the innovations of large institutions, this work has borne great fruit, as illustrated by the fact that the securities industry now widely uses the term "Catholic Investment Screens" to prepare and market new offerings. The Secretariat of the Economy of the Holy See has established its process for developing such guidelines for the Vatican's investment policy. This includes a preliminary process for structural change: renewing the fiduciary scope of governance; reimagining investment strategies; creating standards for partnerships and advisors; and evaluating results on their multiple, integral dimensions. MB builds on this foundational work from many sources, extending the Church's guidance and principles towards good measures for the benefit of all Catholic investors.

> For the very many other instances where ethical investment criteria do not yet exist, MB calls for their immediate development. It offers investors principles and tools for faith-based policies, and a roadmap for implementation.

12. For the very many other instances where ethical investment criteria do not yet exist, MB calls for their immediate development. It offers investors principles and tools for faith-based policies, and a roadmap for implementation.[22] Indeed, given the shared risks from the threats to our common home, every person with financial responsibilities is charged with developing ethical guidelines, with a view to aligning their investment decisions and strategies towards the common good. As challenging as it may be to navigate these often conflicting and sometimes contradictory aims, the role of investing can no longer be divorced from its ethical web of impacts. Pope Benedict XVI asserts that "Development is impossible without upright men and women, without financiers and politicians whose consciences are finely attuned to the requirements of the common good." He explains that we must overcome the "confusion between ends and means, such that the sole criterion for action in business is thought to be the maximization of profit."[23] Indeed, the very objective function

PILLARS OF FAITH: INVESTING IN THE CATHOLIC KEY.

13. The call of MB arrives at an auspicious time. With the world enwrapped in multiple crises,[24] "those who belong to Christ through faith and baptism must confess their baptismal faith,"[25] as "the whole concern of doctrine and its teaching must be directed to the love that never ends."[26] Facing these overlapping crises—which are global as well as local—many managers, financial advisors, and investors recognize that markets have entered a new phase of volatility and uncertainty. MB turns this factual acknowledgement towards its moral implications, which is that—as never before—all humanity, including future generations, are united by a host of entwined vulnerabilities. MB asks, in the *way* of faith, how can these vulnerabilities be heeded and mitigated? In the *truth* of faith, what are the ethical responsibilities to apply to investments? In the *light* of faith, which capacities do we need to grow together as Church to model new economics for integral development?

> Formulating good measures for investing from faith has two primary sources, which MB has mined. One is the *Catechism of the Catholic Church*; the other is the *Compendium of the Social Doctrine of the Church*.

14. Formulating good measures for investing from faith has two primary sources, which MB has mined. One is the *Catechism of the Catholic Church*; the other is the *Compendium of*

the Social Doctrine of the Church. Along with Scripture, these are bedrock for all Catholics, warranting frequent referencing and reflection. Many hands have worked over several years to prepare MB, and these efforts have produced rich summaries from the *Catechism* and *Compendium*. To turn to the urgent task at hand, this call to action provides a précis of those summaries, with richer theological and pastoral materials to follow for more deliberate study.

God's self-revelation as the basis of faith, and for co-commitment to the common good.

15. God is the Creator of all things, who has spoken to humanity through the prophets, and his Son, Jesus Christ. In revealing God's saving love for humanity, God has bequeathed, in the gift of faith, human capacities for discovering in-depth *being in relationship to God, with one another created by the same God*, and *with the rest of creation*. In their dignity every person is therefore relational as well as individual.

- *Call to enquiry and examen*: In the light of faith, the very identity and job-description of the investor are redefined. More than managing transactions strategically and responsibly, investors with faith are invited to regard themselves as immersed in a plurality of relationships. Indeed, the good measure of one's meaning and happiness is from contributing one's life, talents, work and resources to others, and to the world.
- How are today's decisions as an investor specifically cooperating with God's plan for creation and humanity?

Fidelity to God's covenant through Jesus Christ.

16. Jesus enters human history to announce the Reign of God. True God and true man, Jesus's incarnation is—in one

The Principles for *Mensuram Bonam*

sense—the ultimate contradiction, which breaches the assumed divides between the divine and human, between the temporal and the eternal, between death and life. The new order Jesus personifies disrupts the human norms for justice and righteousness. God's love must be made real in all relationships through the love that includes the neighbor, extends to those considered least and last, and even enfolds enemies. Jesus enacts the good measures of God's self-offering, mercy, and forgiveness. And Jesus teaches the good measures, such as with the Beatitudes, for his human sisters and brothers to thrive with the norms of love that humanize justice.

- *Call to vocation*: Investors' choices are fraught with competing and often conflicting priorities, even before applying the lens of faith. This is why Pope Benedict XVI insists on combining faith with reason: to not only "correct the malfunctions" of the economic system, but also "to steer the globalization of humanity in relational terms, in terms of communion and the sharing of goods."[27] Note the practical as well as sacramental dimensions of such collaboration: a communion for ideas, lessons-learned, experiments, best-practices, daring hopes, and to demand together, as a community of faith, more humanizing outcomes.
- Is God's voice—God's call to every person of faith—being heeded? In the tumult of markets, and in the hectic demands of profession, how are moments of prayerful reflection best fashioned?
- A vocational lens changes personal as well as professional perspectives. Pope Benedict XVI "invites contemporary society to a serious review of its lifestyle, which, in many parts of the world, is prone to hedonism and consumerism, regardless of their harmful consequences. What is needed is an effective shift in mentality which can lead

to the adoption of new lifestyles 'in which the quest for truth, beauty, goodness and communion with others for the sake of common growth are the factors which determine consumer choices, savings and investments.'"[28] Are the changes being sought as a faith-based investor aligned with changes in personal lifestyle? How is the investor personally modelling faith and its values?

- Have the values governing and guiding investments been specifically identified and defined? Have the good measures for integrity as a faith-based investor been explicitly clarified? Have the principles or measures for integrality—for considering and respecting the unity of human, social, and ecological inter-relationships—entered into the processes for investment goals and strategies?

Participating in the love and wonder of the Trinity.

17. Catholic imagination and living are formed and informed within the essential, and always new, mystery of the Trinity. Pope Francis stresses that "For Christians, believing in one God who is trinitarian communion suggests that the Trinity has left its mark on all creation."[29] In the imprint of Trinity, faith recognizes a creative potential for unity within diversity. In the imprint of Trinity, the human person, society, and the natural world inhere in one another—an embeddedness that is also a dance; interdependence that is also the font of freedom. In the imprint of Trinity, human persons are summoned to integrity and integrality: to personal wholeness and holiness that is simultaneously relational and responsible for the web of gifts bestowed by the Father, the Son, and the Holy Spirit.

- *Call "to read reality in a Trinitarian key."*[30] Work on responsible investment options has been underway for several decades. At their core the new and multiplying measures attending to environment, society and governance (ESG) reflect a fundamental truth: that the economy is nested within society, impacts human beings in positive and negative ways, and is bound by the natural limits. With a Trinitarian key, the calculus for investors changes from analysis on separate dimensions to loving regard for the whole. As Pope Francis writes, "The divine Persons are subsistent relations, and the world, created according to the divine model, is a web of relationships. Creatures tend towards God, and in turn it is proper to every living being to tend towards other things, so that throughout the universe we can find any number of constant and secretly interwoven relationships."[31]

- As well as considering the existing criteria for social, environmental, and governance dimensions, have the interconnections between them been explored and examined? Are the social and human implications of environmental impacts clear? Who is harmed? Who is advantaged? How is justice strengthened or weakened? Have the ecological impacts of social attitudes or personal consumption been costed? In what ways are corporations or mutual funds influencing governance? Does the lobbying of companies or their influence on regulators align with an investor's purpose and values?

In the embrace of grace.

18. Christian faith reveals that all of human activity finds its fullness in the mercy and love of God, who created human beings in God's image, and redeemed humanity through Jesus Christ. When individuals open themselves to relationship with Christ, the grace received has an impact that abounds and rebounds throughout society and creation. As Jesus took unto himself the fullness of humanity, no human sphere, project, or endeavor is

beyond the reach of God's grace. Nor are prayer and sacraments the only distribution points for grace. Every moment, every task, every decision, is latent with grace from the Holy Spirit for building God's kingdom—for responding to God's great gift of love with our lives. One of the gifts of such grace is for discerning the true value, and therefore measure, of all things.

- *Call to discernment.* Investing with perspective or criteria from faith situates goals and outcomes within God's wondrous grace. Because all investments participate in the bounty of divine gifts, no investment can ever be considered morally neutral. Either God's kingdom is being advanced by the assets being deployed, or it is being neglected and undermined. Many investors and executives acknowledge that the linear calculations limited to "either/or" choices are incomplete, or inadequate. Indeed, the concern for environmental and social impacts bespeaks a turn to "and" thinking—respecting the complexity of the economy as involving the interconnection of multiple factors. Imagining and implementing such an "and" approach is necessary, but also extremely hard. Faith's perspective and grace are indispensable. With faith, the true value of options or outcomes emerges (if we allow it); with grace, innovations or possibilities beyond the scope of current logic breakthrough (if we trust it).
- For the sake of discerning good measures, have the ethical assets and ethical liabilities of investments or strategies been identified? As well as considering positive and negative economic externalities, what—based on facts and qualitative judgements—are the human, social, and ecological assets and liabilities? Are profits 'true' for providing honest, fair and enabling-value to humans and society? Or have harmful impacts been

downloaded on others, or future generations for false profits?

Shaped by the Word of God.

19. The Gospels are the lodestar for Catholic faith—for putting on the mind of Christ, and imitating him in the concrete reality of one's own time and place. The *coming of the Kingdom* Jesus preaches is unfolding still, under the tension of the *here-and-now* and *the-not-yet*; between present and future; between "on earth as it is heaven." Discipleship with Jesus is not limited to following precepts or rituals. It is instead a living friendship by which every person who is baptized participates with Jesus in the daily project of building God's Kingdom. Jesus preaches audacity and patience, an urgent immediacy to take up discipleship and trust that—by God's care—even the smallest of seeds will grow into the largest of trees. Jesus speaks of practical matters such as seeding and planting, and human matters such as herding and hoarding, to expose the contrast between commonplace values and those of God. During his earthly ministry, Jesus' parables frequently invited listeners (and now readers) to immerse themselves in a situation, and allow their own human wisdom to percolate. Those "with eyes to see, and ears to hear" become joyful participants in their personal conversion, combining their human initiatives, creativity, talents, and generosity, with gifts and grace from the Holy Spirit, to contribute to the work of Jesus manifesting God's Kingdom.

- *Call for 'lectio divina.'* As noted, no human domain or experience, including investing, is outside of God's care, or beyond reach of God's grace. In his catechism on prayer, Pope Francis explains both the centrality of Scripture, and its efficacy: "The words of Sacred Scripture were not written to remain imprisoned on papyrus, parchment or paper, but to be received by a

person who prays, making them blossom in his or her heart."³² Reading God's word as prayer, especially when work is busy or times frenetic, "gives us strength and serenity, and even when it challenges us, it gives peace."
- Passages with resonance for investors may include parables such as *The Hidden Treasure, The Pearl of Great Price, and The Net Cast Into the Sea* (Mt. 13:44-49); *The Talents* (Mt. 25:14-30); *The Tenant Farmer* (Mt. 21:33-45); and *The Vineyard Workers* (Mt. 20:1-16).
- The Scriptures, and specifically the Gospels, are not for utility in the linear sense of finding solutions to problems. They are for encountering Jesus and being transformed: as one branch on *The True Vine* (Jn. 15:1-11); becoming *Salt and Light* (Mt. 5:13-16); or serving as *The Yeast* (Lk. 13:20-21). The passages and verses are many; the lessons and inspiration inexhaustible.
- Fidelity is the key. "A passage from Scripture, heard many times already, unexpectedly speaks to me one day and enlightens a situation that I am living. But it is necessary that I be present on that day for that appointment with the Word."³³

With the Holy Spirit. "Abide in my love."

20. In summary, the light of faith illumines a new vision in which the human person recognizes God's loving plan, and appropriates it, in the midst of daily life. So rooted in living faith, one's purpose and sense of meaning permeates all decisions and actions. Saint Paul VI declared in *Populorum progressio* that "The present state of affairs must be confronted boldly, and its concomitant injustices must be challenged and overcome." Indeed, it is the active presence of the Holy Spirit that "has aroused and continues to arouse in man's heart the irresistible requirements of his dignity."³⁴ Hearing God's Word, with heart, mind, and imagination, grows personal integrity to be in alignment with

God's blessings and loving values. With these good measures as our own, we each become indispensable instruments in God's great plan for creation and salvation: *"redeeming and making all things new"* (Rev. 21:5; 2 Cor. 5:17). As many investors have shown, the exercise of financial stewardship with faith's guidance and inspiration can produce not only better results, but also better norms. MB joins this work in progress, celebrating the work begun, learning from best-practices, and inviting collaboration to make processes and measures more robust. As Pope Benedict XVI explains: "earthly activity, when inspired and sustained by charity, contributes to the building of the universal city of God, which is the goal of the history of the human family."[35]

CATHOLIC SOCIAL TEACHING (CST): GOOD MEASURES FOR INVESTOR GUIDANCE AND PRACTICE.

21. Faith in Christ that opens up to the dynamism of God's grace is not simply an intellectual adhesion to revealed truth. To be salvific, it must be formed by charity, as Saint Paul taught *"what matters is faith that makes its power felt through love"* (Gal. 5:6). All along a movement among the faithful to live out the tenets of their faith in society engendered a living tradition in the Church, which now serves as a fount of principles to guide the living of the Christian faith in the world.[36] Faith cannot be a private reality—a set of personal convictions formed from an individual's own doctrine and worship. Faith is incomplete without a vision of the world rooted in God's Word, and without assuming our place in it through our works.[37]

22. A synthesis of the Church's social teaching and tradition is found in the *Compendium of the Social Doctrine of the Church*[38] (CST) and in current papal encyclicals[39] and teaching,[40] as well as in the teachings of Episcopal Conferences. CST draws

upon the gifts of human reason, including insights from philosophy, economics, ecology, the sciences and politics etc. Juxtaposed and brought into synthesis with the teachings of faith and theology, these insights contribute to a social doctrine that places the human person at the center of all world systems of thought and activity.[41] At its heart, CST contributes to the development of human culture which "will develop the whole human person harmoniously and integrally, and will help all men [and women] to fulfill the tasks to which they are called, especially Christians who are fraternally united at the heart of the human family."[42] For the believer then, the Gospel illuminates, deepens and elevates these concepts, giving them a whole new level of meaning in accordance with the person's transcendental nature. This is why Pope Benedict XVI speaks of the impact of faith upon reason, in which "reason always stands in need of being purified by faith." Likewise, he continues "religion always needs to be purified by reason in order to show its authentically human face."[43]

This transcendent vision of the human person, rooted in the Scriptures, is expressed in the principles for *dignity, human rights, the common good, solidarity, subsidiarity and participation, the universal destination of the goods of the earth.*[44] Pope Benedict XVI and Pope Francis have each added new elements to social teaching to illumine current realities with the light of living faith. Concepts of *sustainability, integral ecology, social justice, care for the poor, and care of our common home* have been identified as critical points of reference from the Church's discourses on contemporary issues. All spheres of human activity, including finance, are enmeshed in these issues. With its scope, CST provides investors with tools for proper discernment, making prudent and faith-based decisions for obtaining good value that is also of a wider common good (a *mensuram bonam*). In effect, ROI squared—*return on investment* that contributes a material *return on integral development*.

23. CST's principles (and their application) continue to be refreshed, and enriched. Many aspects of these principles are

well known as they reflect insights from Natural Law. Others warrant study and reflection for the sharpened understanding that subsequent papal teachings have given them.

The Human Person and Human Dignity:[45] The *Personhood* or *Personality* of a human being is the supreme social principle of the Church's social doctrine; and the free development of the human person is the central measure of social order. Created in the image of God (Gen. 1:27), every man, woman and child possesses that dignity in their personhood. Subsequent biblical teaching underscores that dignity is shared by all persons as sisters and brothers regardless of any social or economic distinctions (Eph. 1:5; Rm. 8:29).[46] No person has more intrinsic dignity than the other. By implication, human activity that results in any "deficit in basic human dignity"—such as impoverishment, enslavement, or the privation of freedom—violates the fundamental integrality of God's plan for creation and humanity. Personal progress that realizes human flourishing, well-being, or dignity, must apply to everyone. Each and every person is an end in themselves, never merely an instrument, valued only for utility's sake (such as for production or consumption). True development of human potential only fulfills the norms and demands of *human dignity*[47] when personal capacities are given space and scope to flourish.[48] This universal dimension is not abstract. It means in concrete and practical terms that a person is not *something*, but *someone*.[49] With this God-given dignity, the vocation of every man and woman is to that integral human development[50] which is destined to be fulfilled in authentic love.[51] Freedom is a fundamental expression of this dignity, including those free rights to worship, exercise conscience, and form associations or communities for common purpose. Pope Francis, points to the holy core of human dignity, writing that "humanity is the 'sacred temple' in which 'merchants' are prevented from speculating," and which "may not be reduced to serving money."[52]

The Common Good: The principle of common good, "to which every aspect of social life must be related if it is to attain its fullest meaning," stems from the dignity, unity and equality of all people and safeguards it.[53] The common good indicates "the sum total of social conditions which allow people, either as groups or as individuals, to reach their fulfillment more fully and more easily."[54] A powerful synonym for the common good is what Popes Paul VI, Benedict XVI and Francis call "integral human development." By extension in today's reality, Pope Francis asserts that "an integral ecology is inseparable from the notion of the common good, a central and unifying principle of social ethics."[55] Perhaps as never before, we can witness each of us personally that the good of every human is intertwined with the natural good—that fulfilling personal capabilities, achieving security and hope for families, and growing resilient communities and institutions—are interrelated as a singular ecology. Every group or community shares responsibility within this ecology of abounding mutuality to ensure that conditions guarantee the personal, familial and associative good of its members.[56] Dignified life for realizing one's full and personal integral development is integrally connected to others and to nature. Aristotle envisioned basic ethical interpenetration.[57] Saint John XXIII made the same affirmation from faith with his call for a "modern welfare state" that ensures social security, and provides assistance to those who cannot otherwise afford full participation in the goods of the community.[58] For the pontiff, the measure of governance is the vitality of the common good. He stipulated that every society should have persons "invested with public authority" to "take account of all those social conditions which favour the full development of the human personality."[59]

In continuity with this teaching, Pope Francis calls for "states and civil institutions that…are primarily concerned with individuals and the common good"[60] which are rooted in social friendship and social charity.[61] When the economy loses its human face, then people become servants to money.[62] Pope Francis elaborates that "this is a form of idolatry against which we are called to react by reestablishing the rational order of things." With the common good as the norm, "money must serve, not rule."[63]

Solidarity: Relational obligations to care for common interests engender solidarity. This principle is rooted in essential fraternity of the human family, with its consequence of living for and with social love.[64] Solidarity is an active commitment to work together, sharing gifts and applying conscience to the challenges of securing harmony and hope for the common good to be fruitful. According to Pope Francis, "gestures of generosity, solidarity and care well up within us, because we were made for love."[65] Indeed, solidarity may well entail a sense of compassion, but it is much more. Saint John Paul II described it as "a firm and persevering determination to commit oneself to the common good; that is to say, to the good of all and of each individual, because we are all really responsible for all…"[66] Solidarity is an act of inclusion and belonging, which ensures and defends the conditions for everyone's free participation in the common work of society.[67] The economy and investments, whether conscious or not, depend on the social trust which only the common good generates. Solidarity is therefore a lens for evaluating our gestures of interrelatedness, including initiatives such as corporate social responsibility or ethical investing. Similarly to trust, solidarity is fragile—easily taken for granted or neglected. Ultimately, by nature of humanity's shared dignity, no one is exempt from fulfilling personal responsibility towards the common good of other persons and of creation (i.e. integral ecology).

Social Justice: Effective care for common interests hinges on justice, and especially from the integral realization and support of social justice. What is known as 'general justice' (described as commutative, or legal) regulates relationships by setting and enforcing the law. Such rules provide crucial safeguards for rights in the exercise of contracts, enforcing utility and protecting ownership. Social justice moves beyond obligatory compliance to include the moral norms and ideals relating to the shared concern for integral potential. Informed by God's overarching vision of justice and mercy, it opens up that expansive justice beyond the letter of the law that is needed to realize new horizons for inclusion based on solidarity and love.[68] Pope Benedict XVI observed that the market is subject to the principles of so-called commutative justice. Giving and receiving between parties is regulated as merely a transaction. The social doctrine of the Church unceasingly highlights the importance of adapting market and economic functions to include distributive justice and social justice. Why? Because markets participate in a wider network of relations and public goods. If governed solely by principles of contractual equivalence in the value of exchanged goods, it cannot produce on its own the social cohesion required for efficiency and synergy. Distributive justice is not charity. It cannot be left only to philanthropy. All involved in governance, especially in politics, but also in all other spheres of society, are charged with contributing to social justice to renew and grow common good. The good measure here involves giving precedence to the disadvantaged—by redistribution—so that everyone is accorded the dignity of being included.[69]

Subsidiarity: Persons deserve the dignity of being protagonists for their own growth and well-being. Whatever one's status—whether worker or refugee, student or caregiver, professional or migrant worker—every person warrants the dignity of being seen and heard to help shape their own destiny. Subsidiarity is the commitment to enable persons to exercise influence and choice within the social decision-making closest to their own lived reality. This principle fulfills freedom's basic norm of agency. It is imperative because "every person, family and intermediate group has something original to offer to the community."[70] Hence the worth of each person is tangibly appreciated when enabled to actively participate in the common social agenda.[71] *Subsidiarity* requires due care and respect from

The Principles for *Mensuram Bonam*

larger and more remote entities, to nurture the personal initiative, freedom and responsibility for smaller, more local entities to assume the dignity of responsibility for their decisions.

Subsidiarity is much more than simple *delegation*, which often allows the larger body-politic or corporation to retain power and ultimate control. When delegated-to, persons are accountable to leaders or superiors or managers for outcomes. *Solidarity* distributes roles and power horizontally, creating mutual accountability from all levels towards the common good. In fact, there is a deep correlation between the moral authority entrusted to leaders and the agency achieved through *subsidiarity*. Leaders of large organizations give expression to the social possibilities simmering in the common good, and they set vision as well as parameters for governance. However, the authority and credibility of that leadership pivots on equipping local entities and individuals to assume risks and responsibility. *Subsidiarity* flourishes in a two-way flow within hierarchies: providing the feedback to leaders that facilitates setting purpose and principles for social relations, while providing capabilities to those persons closer to the ground level who contribute implementation and innovation.

Care for Our Common Home: The environmental sensibilities now inscribed on global consciousness are a social awakening to the long-ago revealed truths about God's creation in the sacred Scriptures. There are two creation narratives in Genesis. In the first, God creates humankind "in the image of God he created them; male and female he created them" (Gen. 1:27). Instantly, God conferred two blessings on the first humans, with each blessing incurring corresponding obligations. Adam and Eve were told, "Be fruitful and multiply, fill the earth and subdue it." And they were given "dominion" over all the creatures and living organisms on the earth, including seeds for food and fruit (Gen. 1:28-30). Entrusted by God with these blessings, Adam and Eve had to work the earth to produce the necessities for their lives, while protecting the productive capacity of the earth to serve future generations. All the dimensions of what we now call sustainability were fashioned within those first obligations bequeathed to our first parents. With those moral precedents, sustainability assumes a sacramental dimension, correcting the unlimited exploitation of an economy premised on growth without respect for limits.[72] Caring for our common home, for example, with less consumption or fewer personal experiences, opens two possibilities: for those with more, to savor what they have with appreciation; and for persons with much less, to access their fair share of God's bounty as a dignity-bearing member of the human family living in a common planetary home.

The earth is not a dead resource. It is a living organism with untold creatures and materials in constant flow to serve life. Saint Francis of Assisi had a keen sense for nature's holiness, preaching to birds, and enjoining trees and other creatures to join him in thanksgiving praise to God the Creator. In his Canticle of the Creatures he called our planet "Sweet, Mother earth."[73]

Inclusion of the Most Vulnerable: God's self-revelation and covenant have always emerged in specific promises and consolations offered to those at the margins—the poor, the suffering, and the most vulnerable. In Exodus "the Israelites groaned under their slavery, and cried out. Out of their slavery their cry for help rose up to God. God heard their groaning and God remembered his covenant with Abraham, Isaac, and Jacob" (2:23-24). Throughout her history, the Church has emphasized that the measures for the common good, and for justice, are inextricably connected to the dignity, respect, and inclusion accorded to the least powerful. In *Evangelii gaudium*, his first Apostolic Exhortation, Pope Francis stresses this fundamental concern: "Our faith in Christ, who became poor, and was always close to the poor and the outcast, is the basis of our concern for the integral development of society's most neglected members."[74] Extending "the option for the poor" is, therefore, "a theological category"—a tenet of faith that sparks conscience in politics, culture, and economics. The inclusion of the most vulnerable cannot be simply a matter of charity or philanthropy. Even the best human systems are fallible for being human, and even the most informed decisions are limited by the imperfections of the available information. Inevitably, structural distortions result which privilege power and either implicitly or explicitly exclude those at the margins. Today's most pressing example is that many of the communities around the world that are suffering first the calamitous effects of climate change are those that least contributed to human-caused global warming. Resolving inequality, and generating inclusion, pivot on a corresponding asymmetry of care towards the vulnerable, which, paradoxically, helps the Church as a whole learn and live the true message of Christ's Gospel.[75]

Integral Ecology: As mentioned previously, both Pope Benedict XVI and Pope Francis have addressed the ever-more pressing realities of the ecological crisis by introducing the innovative social teachings relating to "integral ecology." The near meltdown of the global financial system disintegrated much of the unity that was promised by globalization. It turned out that vast innovations for the global capacities for finance and trade failed to develop a corresponding maturity in ethics. Globalization, as Pope Benedict XVI observes, has made us neighbours without making us brothers and sisters.[76] Markets recovered quickly from the crisis, while inequality became more acute. This gap, compounded by 'hyper-individualism,' is an affront to the underlying inter-connectedness of society and creation. Pope Benedict writes: "The Book of Nature is one and indivisible: it takes in not only the environment but also life, sexuality, marriage, the family, social relations: in a word, integral human development."[77] The typology from this teaching is decisive: the human person is only whole in relation to others in society, and society is only whole from the natural ecology that is its host. Pope Francis adds that integral ecology is a conviction which embraces and emphasizes the inter-relatedness of all things.[78] Thus, integral ecology calls for "an 'economic ecology' capable of appealing to a broader vision of reality."[79] Ultimately, then, integral ecology serves to broaden the scope and vision of the application of the common good to all that is encompassed by care for our common home.[80] The ethical challenge attends to the many dimensions of integrality, while resisting the "danger constituted by utopian and ideological visions" of the human person and nature.[81]

The CST principles in which the recommendations of MB are rooted inspire a *solidarity-based commitment*. This entails promoting not only returns, but also human dignity, care for creation and inclusive growth through united action bound by love.[82] Consequently, these principles are much more than a mere checklist. Each has a fulsome integrity, requiring reflection and discernment.

24. Of interest to all human beings, CST has three particular resonances for investors.

One is to escape "fiduciary absolutism"; the enclosed logic of financial engineering focused exclusively on short-term gains, which rejects any ethical accountability even as it commoditizes human persons, social goods, and God's gift of creation. With the guidance of the Gospel and CST, MB seeks to restore fiduciary duty to its original commission (still recognized in many jurisdictions), that is, to exercise the ethical concerns that fulfill terms of trust and the duty to care.

- *Call to re-set vision and responsibilities.* For investors, the implications of this fiduciary reset will have implications for governance, including the scope for investment boards, the training for directors or trustees, and the ethical priorities to demand from regulators and securities issuers.

Another resonance or implication is to use faith-based measures to animate from ethics the many movements in society

The Principles for *Mensuram Bonam*

and the economy advocating change. As noted, much progress has been made in the last several decades to adjust to crises that affect all human beings. Religious orders and institutions have been at the forefront of these changes. With MB, the role now is to broaden the base for applying the wisdom of faith to the complicated questions investors are now confronting.

- *Call to develop and deepen best-responsibility practices.* For investors, the implications are twofold: to ensure that investment vision, strategy, processes, and risk assessments apply the most up-to-date norms from ever-developing responsibility initiatives; and to collaborate with others to enrich these multi-dimensional investment screens with questions and good measures from faith.

A third use of CST is to cast the hopes and measures for an as-yet-unborn society and economy towards what is practically needed for humanity and its cultures to thrive. Today's paradigm for change remains locked in the imagination it is trying to transcend: trust is valued as "social capital;" persons as "human capital;" ideas or innovations as "intellectual capital:" arts and beauty as "cultural capital;" wisdom as "experiential capital;" with religious and ethic values as "moral capital." By implication of these measures, all that is inestimable in God's creation, including humanity's capacity to love and create, are reduced to a single measure of utility. True sustainability and justice requires the genius of financial capital, but as a service to humanity and not as its only or definitive measure.[83]

- *Call to imagine what is needed—and what is possible—for integral human development.* For investors, the implications involve a fundamental shift in perspective. Even if only briefly or tentatively, the task is to work-back from the vision faith-principles engender, rather than trying to catch the status quo up to them. Experiments for ethical insight matter, including making space in any portfolio for ethical Research & Development (R&D)—initiatives that apply values as the antecedent to value.

25. For the task at hand—to summon action, and provide preliminary guidance—MB provides a preliminary summary, with each row providing the core principle, its implications, and preliminary questions for investors:

CST Principles	Implications for Investment	Questions for Discernment
The Human Person and Human Dignity	• The human person, in their embodiment and dignity, is the measure for all social, economic and political development. • As a human activity, investments are never neutral. Integral development is either being advanced or fractured.	• Is human freedom enhanced or degraded? • Are human rights fully respected? • Are opportunities fair and equally accessible? • Are negative externalities borne fairly by the beneficiaries?
The Common Good	• Rights and opportunities for integral development spring from the common good, which is depleted or destroyed if not replenished by duties undertaken with charity.	• Are social values uplifted or neglected? • How specifically does the community benefit? • Is others' participation included or excluded? • Are persons' capabilities allowed to thrive?
Solidary	• By their dignity and talents, every person has an indispensable role in God's plan for creation and salvation. Solidarity opens participation—enabling each to contribute to what is needed to thrive together.	• Are other persons respected or commodified? • Is the social impact unifying or divisive? • How is nature's bounty valued and preserved for future generations? • Will this investment grow or fray social trust?

Continued

The Principles for *Mensuram Bonam*

Social Justice	• To inspire and sustain justice requires more than mere equivalence. To fulfill its social aim and God-granted scope, justice must invest and redistribute surplus capacities to create conditions that best seed and sustain human hopes.	• How will inequality be ameliorated? • Are stakeholders heard and heeded? • Have the excluded, the most vulnerable, or those at the margins been recognized and respected? • Are the expected outcomes ethically inspiring?
Subsidiarity	• Retaining human scale, exercising responsibility at the local or community level where policy meets the exigencies of practice. • Delegating authority to widen decision-making, allowing participants the dignity of their own duties for the common good.	• Does governance empower community-level decisions? • Are risks mapped to include social and local threats or implications? • Does governance accountability engender widespread social harmony? • Have those most impacted had their say?
Care for Our Common Home	• Human beings share the earth with other species along with future generations. People have always relied on the goodness of the planet for sustenance and creaturely need. As we now better appreciate from ecological sciences, humans are embedded in an intricate and fragile web of interdependences that requires consciousness and care.	• Is authentic sustainability being realized (and "greenwashing" avoided)? • How are investment strategies managing the trade-off between long-term sustainability and short-term returns? • How is the stewardship entrusted by God being fulfilled? • Are the innovations for a new, more responsible paradigm being seeded and supported?
The Inclusion of the Most Vulnerable	• Human systems are imperfect, creating conditions throughout history that either exclude, penalize or marginalize the poor. • Precious to God, the most vulnerable are the standard for evaluating the efficacy of justice, and the dignity shared in solidarity and in participating in the common good.	• Do investment policies include lessons from the marginalized? • Beyond "trickle-down," which benefits accrue to those at the margins of power? • How are structural distortions or exclusions that impact the most vulnerable addressed? • Do portfolios include R&D to advance inclusion?

Continued

Integral Ecology	• Each person receives life and dignity as gifts from God. These form persons for relationship on multiple levels: with family; within community; with colleagues and society, and with the air, water, food and sustenance of the earth. Immersed in these gifts, the person's vocation is to become "more human."	• How is the whole human person affected? Are social relations strengthened or weakened? • Are the criteria of integral development met in its human, social, and ecological dimensions? • Are quantitative and qualitative metrics providing systemic inputs for evaluating results? • What do we owe future generations—for their sustainability, dignity, and common good?

26. Several considerations are to be underscored regarding these principles and summaries. One is that the principles are framed for relevance to investors yet using terms and themes from Catholic living tradition. For example, the "interdependence" modifying "the common good" is from Saint John Paul II; the principle of giving precedence to those most vulnerable (long a teaching of the Church) has been emphasized anew by Pope Francis as caring for, and learning from, those at the margins. Importantly, this summary is but a starting point—a preliminary reference for reflecting on the principles for investing with faith. Hopefully, this will spark more questions and dialogue among the many people (both Catholic, and not) who are striving to evolve new standards and practices for investing.

27. Even while appreciating the quality of each principle, it is important to recognize that CST works as a system. Each principle is at once indispensable yet incomplete without the moral bearings from the others. For example, the dignity of the person cannot be segregated from the common good, nor come to fulfillment without the mutual potential unleashed by solidarity. And integral ecology is, at once, a local and global priority. It necessitates a subsidiarity rooted in one's local place, as well

The Principles for *Mensuram Bonam*

as a recognition that natural degradation undermines justice for those most vulnerable to the adverse consequences now and in the future. Today's economic and social problems are seen as involving extreme complexity. CST's principles are by nature a system—a multi-part method for moral evaluation that honors complexity's trials and creative potential.

28. Measuring dignity or vulnerability is as vexing as formulating definitive metrics for sustainability. However, we know these qualities intimately as human persons—from our own lives and souls. Human common sense, enlivened by sense from faith in the Incarnated Son of God, provides qualitative norms that can effectively anticipate quantitative metrics. The combined impact of any investment may be generally assessed by how they avoid harm (upholding life) and enhance humanity (dignity); are of benefit to society (promoting the common good, justice, peace, harmony, growth); and contribute to resolving the pressing issues that societies face (hunger, conflicts, sickness, inequalities, education etc.). Using some of the tools that have recently been developed in the Impact Investing sector is a starting point.[84] CST provides an ethical complement to these important tools, while turning investors also towards models from faith that technical methodologies alone cannot fathom.

> CST provides an ethical complement to these important tools, while turning investors also towards models from faith that technical methodologies alone cannot fathom.

29. While MB's good measures are focused primarily on investments in the capital markets, they apply as well to all investments that imitate God's original initiative to vest Eve and Adam—to take to heart the vulnerability of the other. Pope Francis' call for the Church to serve as a "field hospital"[85] is an example of such investing, literally and ethically dressing

humanity's most damaging wounds from poverty and exclusion. Investing with the good measures of faith is by definition polyvalent: investing in prayer and reflection; investing in learning, especially from non-financial sources; investing in inclusion; investing in listening and dialogue; investing in compassion and understanding for the stranger; and investing in dreams which seem improbable from foresight yet are essential in hindsight.

Chapter II

THE PRACTICAL GUIDANCE FROM *MENSURAM BONAM*

30. The principles identified in Chapter 1, with their implications and questions, are an animating benchmark for faith-consistent, faith-guided investing. Such principles work towards an immediate practical application, while, at the same time, generating momentum for the movement towards new finance that is intrinsically ethical. In fact, the prophetic imperatives of faith are, at this time, increasingly aligned with the needs for social justice and ecological sustainability sought by experts in multiple spheres. Many in the economic mainstream accept that ethics are needed, especially for just and sustainable outcomes, however, as yet with little progress in transforming the overall purpose of economic activity. All too often ethics remain optional, or a constraint to address, while managing the maximization of other outcomes. Realigning economics-with-ethics can no longer be ignored, or delayed. Pope Francis underscores this point: "It is not enough to balance, in the medium term, the protection of nature with financial gain, or the preservation of the environment with progress. Halfway measures simply delay the inevitable disaster."[86] MB aims for a new investing culture that melds technical expertise with faith's moral guidance. If similar to the innovations the financial industry has been seeking—with its

numerous responsibilities products such as ESG—the key from MB is that ethics resonant with Catholic faith are now crucial to the objective function of investing.

> "Business activity is essentially a noble vocation, directed to producing wealth and improving our world... Business abilities, which are a gift from God, should always be clearly directed to the development of others and to eliminating poverty, especially through the creation of diversified work opportunities."
>
> Pope Francis, *Fratelli Tutti*, 123

31. MB speaks to all Catholic investors. As institutional investors will have very different questions, aims, and resources than individuals, each, in their own way, can use MB to bring faith-qualities to existing practices. Each choice contributes to scaling-up faith-based investing. Beyond sharing guidance and inviting reflection, the hope is that MB will be the basis for dialogue and deepened analysis—for groups and communities to study and question together the shared project of integral human development. Other religions have provided their faith perspective regarding markets and the economy. Many groups from across faiths are in dialogue about these globally shared urgencies and opportunities.[87] With so much to learn together, MB adds to this ongoing conversation the social teaching that Catholics have gleaned from their faith and Natural Law.

32. According to Pope Francis, the immediate task before us is twofold: to address with concrete measures "the hidden pandemics of this world, the pandemics of hunger and violence and climate change;" and to heed God's call in our time "to dare to create something new."[88] Investors have a crucial role in this dreaming and doing, applying their faith, imagination, love and

The Practical Guidance from *Mensuram Bonam*

expertise in pursuit and service of an ethically integral economy. The material that follows is only a starting point, meant neither to be exhaustive nor definitive. It first offers steps for getting started for those personal investors or small institutions seeking to build a foundation for faith-consistent investing (FCI). What comes after are more detailed lessons for advancing faith-based practices from larger Catholic institutional investors. Real decisions made by investors, asset owners, and asset managers can amplify the well-being of the human family, looking beyond financial returns to also care for society and creation to benefit everyone—including future generations.

GETTING STARTED: ADOPTING A FAITH-BASED PROCESS.

33. In one sense, CST is like a GPS with faith, providing a map—a view from above—with guideposts and suggestions for navigating a difficult route. Changing the horizon or culture for investment is never easy. Learning and unlearning are needed, to shift assumptions and expectations, and to begin re-setting each of the steps in an investor's process with the due-diligence from faith. Pope Francis has introduced a methodology for reading the signs of the times that can be also fruitfully applied to the exigencies of faith-consistent investing. His three steps are contemplate, discern, and propose. Contemplation is for prayerful immersion in the issue at hand—for taking stock of complexities and confusion, allowing emotions and intellect to be informed within the push and pull between anguish and hope. The prayer here is not for resolution or results, but to humbly allow truth to emerge and be encountered. Discernment gives honest attention to the paradoxical forces, and even contradictory ones, that characterize human life. More than mere rational analysis, discernment involves a willing openness to new alternatives based

on "God's motives, invitation, and will." In Pope Francis' words: "ideas are debated, but reality is discerned." As the word itself suggests, Propose is a recommendation that is not yet fixed or complete. Insights from contemplation and creative innovations from discernment conjure action that is, itself, new and therefore a fount for learning and testing.[89]

34. For investors beginning this journey, the key is to set aside time for honest examination—to interrogate practices and assumptions, and to formulate the terms that are applicable for faith-consistent investing. Not every aim, nor every quandary, will be resolved. The priority is to start, using preliminary deliberations and decisions to keep learning—to keep growing capacities for aligning investments to faith. That process may include:

- Formulating an *Investment Policy Statement*, which identifies the chosen governing principles from faith, and sets the horizon for investments. Setting or re-setting such a policy brings faith considerations into direct conversation with an investor's priorities, risk tolerance, return objectives, and time horizon. In effect, this serves as a proactive "balance sheet," identifying moral as well as financial assets or aims, and liabilities or risks. (See the table in Chapter 1, 25).
- With this *Policy* as a guide, risk parameters are revised to reflect both financial conditions and ethical expectations. This framework for risks in their multiple dimensions becomes the pivot on which to base a prudent construction of financial portfolios.
- Specifically identifying values, both to reflect the tolerance for risk, and the degree of urgency for realizing faith-consistent outcomes. The usual investment norms of prudence and due-diligence are, in this case, required in full; enlarged to include more of the ethical considerations that impact choices and results.

The Practical Guidance from *Mensuram Bonam*

- Importantly with faith-consistent goals, the very system for investment reasoning is reset. Questions and criteria for performance impact investment strategies, and become a filter for evaluation options and results. Small changes can make a big difference, particularly as they combine with others' efforts to implement faith-consistent investing.
- Faith-consistent criteria thus allow investors to make more precise decisions about assets, securities, properties, issuers, and other fund options. These criteria also guide participation in affecting market players and performance through engagement, enhancement, and exclusions. (More regarding these processes is detailed below in 39.)
- Monitoring progress is crucial for fulfilling authentic fiduciary duty, realizing security and sustainability, while aligning with the vision and values of faith. The monitoring also takes stock of learning, to strengthen the faith-guided investment process, and to build capacity for future investments.

Modes of financial management and economic commerce may, naturally, vary from region to region, and from investor to investor. Not all large investors have yet adopted this process. Small investors, or those managing personal assets, will also bring varying degrees of expertise or resources to these questions. Faith-consistent investing is a trajectory rather than a fixed recipe or accomplishment. This is why the lessons from those larger Catholic institutions that have wrestled with faith-consistent investing are germane to all investors. In building such an investment approach, several different routes may be selected by investors or asset owners. MB describes some of them below. As referenced in Chapter 1, various Bishops' conferences and some Vatican bodies have also issued much more detailed sets of rules that can also be accessed for reference and inspiration (See 25).

> Faith-consistent investing is a trajectory rather than a fixed recipe or accomplishment. This is why the lessons from those larger Catholic institutions that have wrestled with faith-consistent investing are germane to all investors.

LESSONS FROM CATHOLIC INNOVATORS.

35. As noted, Church and Catholic institutions have been spearheading evaluative approaches for applying the insights and imperatives from faith to their investment strategies and practices. The lessons gleaned from these years of experience have implications for all investors of faith.

Any Catholic institution that is entrusted with resources to fulfill its mission faces a dual responsibility:

- A professional duty to manage those resources prudently and to carefully fund programs, projects and tasks through which its mission is realized.
- A moral duty that, to the best of their ability, they use the tenets of faith and CST to align their investment and management practices with God's great plan (for integral human development).

In their faithful, competent, social and morally responsible stewardship of the Church's resources, those who hold these responsibilities are joining (with) the efforts of believers who have for centuries sought to integrate their beliefs into their lives and their business activities.[90] For institutions and

The Practical Guidance from *Mensuram Bonam*

their governing bodies to be faithful to this responsibility, they need to give thoughtful and regular consideration to modes of incorporating the extensive tradition of CST into investment decisions, with the intention of witnessing to the love of Christ and benefiting the common good of the global community. So doing, they make the outcome of their activities truly a *mensuram bonam*—a good measure.

36. While some Catholic asset owners are just beginning to discover the moral demands flowing from faith in their investing decisions, others have already adopted principles and practices. Appropriate to their unique situation, these investors have benefited from the research, operational advancements, and the many tools that have been developed in the fields of faith-based and socially responsible investing. With this solid foundation for authentic fiduciary responsibility, they have carefully focused on investment opportunities that avoid superficial or marketing-led options.

37. Taking standard practices to the next level, the strategy for a faith-based approach must first be described in an *investment policy statement*. As outlined above (in 34), this *policy* should be drawn up by any person in charge of managing those assets as a way of defining an investor's priorities, risk tolerance, return objectives and time horizon. This may depend on the laws and regulations that are in place in different jurisdictions concerning ownership, capital deployment and transfer, on the vehicles and types of funds available to investors or on the skills of those given oversight of the asset or portfolio. As a result, these structures may affect the mode of applying faith-consistent investing procedures and criteria, hopefully without frustrating that effort.

38. Many instruments can be used for FCI or faith-aligned investing. Direct holding in listed securities is one possible investment choice. Equity or fixed income mutual funds (and/or ETFs[91]) can also provide the right tool. Mutual funds attentive to

the needs of socially responsible investors, or responsive to CST and its integral development objectives, are growing in number, although viable options are still limited or may apply only to certain segments of the investment portfolio or may not be available in all countries.[92] Because the work of developing appropriate tools and approaches in this field continues to evolve, Catholic asset owners must monitor these developments, while actively encouraging those responsible for this research. For those market segments in which satisfactory mutual fund options that formally address CST are not available, mutual funds may be differentiated by a review of mutual fund holdings in terms of the level of exposure to areas of concern or areas of positive investment as well as the proxy voting policy. In addition, in recent years, impact investing, ESG investing and program-related investing have presented Catholic asset owners with new diverse and multiple approaches and options (although there are some ongoing efforts to try and bring more global coherence to that which ESG exactly refers to). New tools that can be integrated into their investment programs can simultaneously address some critical social and environmental challenges that society faces towards making outcomes truly beneficial and integral.

39. Determining how an investment integrates CST principles can be challenging. Information is often incomplete or unavailable. Claims are often difficult to validate. Nevertheless, this must not discourage investors from considering ethical investments in those portions of a diversified portfolio where options are available. In some cases, uncertainty about potential concerns relative to the faith-based or ethical nature of an investment opportunity may lead the investor to conclude that the investment needs to be avoided. Faith-based institutions have chartered many of these waters. Using the core tenets of faith, they use CST principles to set and refine the ethical direction for investing. With this faith-consistent framework they then navigate the options, such as those among ESG or best-

The Practical Guidance from *Mensuram Bonam*

in-class offerings, to select stocks and bonds. This process and these criteria (detailed in 41 and the *Call to Action* that follows) can also be applied, with some degree of difficulty, in decision-making about other asset classes. When options are confusing or unclear, MB encourages discernment in prayer, along with flexibility and creativity in making investment decisions that are faith-compliant and reflect CST. As challenging as this may be, the innovations for realizing faith-inspired investments are part of the vocation of investing. In turn, this effort may also open up new pathways for other faith-minded investors, shifting the center of gravity to ever-more responsible investments.

40. It is often assumed that mixing faith and ethics with investment criteria may compromise returns. Such concerns have largely been refuted. When faith and ethics criteria are developed with the adequate levels of consideration and expertise, there should be little to no fear of underperformance, or of the risk of not meeting one's fiduciary responsibility.[93] Indeed, there is a growing acknowledgement that responsible investing can deliver equal or better ultimate performance (*mensuram bonam*) over the long term: do well by doing good! To not consider the financial value of environmental, social, and governance issues, is in fact a risk. Neglecting ethical innovations in the market may cause investors to lose the opportunity to improve their risk-adjusted returns, and, therefore, to deliver better overall value for their stakeholders. By example, after the financial market crisis in 2020 caused by the Covid-19 pandemic, sustainable market indices outperformed non-sustainable peers. Ethical researchers have also shown that in times of downturn, the most trusted companies suffered fewer losses than the market average, and recovered faster as conditions improved.[94] This can be referred to as a *Sustainability Premia*.

41. When Catholic asset owners work to adopt faith-formed and faith-consistent investing policies to apply across all asset classes, they are to be attentive to the immediate, long-term and

collateral impacts that their holdings may have upon people, communities, the climate and the earth, "our common home." Once again, the issues of investment governance must be underscored. The complexity of asset management choices with various responsibility screens requires specific skills. It may be that a dedicated group (an investment committee) may be formed or convened to provide an advisory function for the investment policy of the individual institution. To leverage scale, opportunities may be pursued to better coordinate investment and debt policies between Catholic institutions, at a national or even international level (including Vatican and Holy See entities). With cooperation and consistency, such a network of specialists will become a reliable and effective resource for evaluating from faith-criteria new investment proposals and developments throughout the financial sector.

FAITH-CONSISTENT INVESTING (FCI) IN PRACTICE.

42. MB does not prescribe any one approach to investing. Evolving rapidly, the structures, priorities and options for responsible investing are very much a work in progress. FCI provides the clarity from values for finding the best way through competing or confusing options. Assuring such faith-consistency is itself a living process of learning, collaboration, and decision-making. It requires commitments for engaging others, enhancing current offerings and future innovations, while excluding those investment options that violate the Church's teachings. Each of these—engagement, enhancement, and exclusion—involve deliberation from faith as well as practical action.

- *Call to engage.* The goal of the engagement process is for investors to actively leverage their ownership to

The Practical Guidance from *Mensuram Bonam*

influence—through dialogue, mutual learning, and collaboration—the enterprises in which they invest. Usually, this means creating greater alignment between operations, not only in relation to the relevant international legal and ethical standards, but also for coherence with the spirit of CST principles. Dialogue gives substance to solidarity, according participants the dignity of being heard on issues of mutual concern, such as the common good or the integral ecology. Active engagement is therefore an indispensable element in any faith-consistent investment policy. When carefully organized and strategically managed, the dialogue from engagement can lead to constructive and inspiring improvements. Catholic asset owners and investors may also extend this dialogue—inviting and motivating others, especially believers—to support the proposals that offer an opportunity to achieve professional results that accord with the ethos of their faith. Engagement in this sphere requires the same time and patience as any other cultural or structural change. Even companies that respond positively to active dialogue from faith-criteria will need time to understand the issue in depth, and develop their own strategic justification.

Engagement involves a variety of strategies, including what have been called 'vote, voice and exit':

- In the case of public companies, shareholders can actively exercise the responsibilities of their co-ownership with regard to the policies and practices of the enterprise by voting their shares and participating in the annual general meeting (the 'vote' strategy).
- Investors can also engage in dialogue with those in responsible management positions within an enterprise

in order to advance changes at financial and non-financial levels (the 'voice' strategy).
- If these strategies have no prospects for success in the long term, divestment strategies should be discussed as a final step and corresponding decisions should be exercised (the 'exit' strategy).

Direct engagement or active shareholding should be undertaken where and when judged appropriate by asset owners. Decisions about specific activities need to be considered within the context of the investment policies and objectives. To maximize influence, engagement is best exercised collaboratively—working together with other investors (faith-based and socially responsible)—or transferring responsibility for active dialogue to financial service providers who specialize in engagement. As always, prudence is required to select the right provider who is qualified in terms of experience and scale, is affordable and accountable, and will work according to the policy and values set by those responsible for engagement strategies. These providers exercise engagement as proxies for their customers and clients, either independently or in conjunction with other players at various levels, from exerting voting rights, speaking at annual meetings or directly approaching those responsible within the enterprises. Their voice is heard in particular when they credibly raise specific questions about the policies or products or activities of an enterprise.

- *Call to enhance.* The *enhancing policy* for positive investments in light of the CST adopts a proactive stance regarding the contributions or potential of funds or enterprises to those environmental, social, human goods needed for integral development. Among the considerations to be evaluated are the relationships with workers, suppliers, customers, communities,

The Practical Guidance from *Mensuram Bonam*

stakeholders and partners as well as shareholders. Metrics and reporting are useful tools for implementing the enhancing policy towards more positive investments. This commitment to *enhance* begins by identifying social objectives, including for resolving or correcting issues such as job insecurity, poor access to health, lack of food or water security, and corruption. The good measure can be discerned by itemizing and exploring in depth the principles from CST (such as the human person and dignity, or the common good, etc.) which apply most directly or urgently to the task at hand. Helpful here are the implications and questions for discernment outlined in the CST principles and matrix (above in 23, 24, and 25). Importantly, particular attention must not only focus on the current situation, but also recognize what is unfolding—taking into account transition paths already underway, or analyzing 'watch-lists' for the initial phase for the so-called mixed investments. Lessons and rankings from various responsibility-initiatives, whether from categories such as *impact investing*, *best-in-class*, or *ESG*, may help formulate or guide the investor's *enhancing policy*. Without presuming to be definitive, the commitment to *enhancing* may involve:

i) Impact investing is guided by a vision and mission that seek to respond to different social and environmental challenges confronting communities and society. It is one viable option available in this category, and shows promise as an effective tool to help investors move beyond the negative screens for "do no evil" or "avoid harm." Rather than simply wait for innovative developments to emerge, *impact investing* aims to spark and advance projects that particularly align with faith. In effect, portfolios that include a type of R&D investment in social or cause-driven enterprises. As Pope Benedict XVI underscores, "Efforts are needed—and it is essential to say this—not only to create "ethical" sectors or segments of the economy or the world of finance, but to ensure that the whole economy—the whole of finance—is ethical, not merely by virtue of an external label, but by its respect for requirements intrinsic to its very nature. The Church's social teaching is quite clear on the subject, recalling that the economy, in all its branches, constitutes a sector of human activity."[95]

- Based on mission or other values-formed goals, Catholic practitioners of *impact investing* identify a set of themes, issues, challenges, or categories to channel investments towards promoting integral human development and the common good. These goals are refined using the lens of CST and are often guided by the experience of other practitioners in the field. The effectiveness of such impact-driven investing depends on robust and transparent methodologies for evaluation, including demands for ever-more detailed and validated metrics.
- Positive and proactive social and environmental *impact investing strategies* have always been considered a part of faith-based commitments, chosen because their specific objective is to contribute to the promotion of the universal common good or the care of creation.

ii) The "best-in-class approach" draws guidance and inspiration from faith-consistent innovators. As with the *enhance* strategy, this often means coupling validated impact-investing or ESG criteria with the interrelated human, social, and natural factors that constitute the "integral ecology"[96] to assess and rank issuers of shares and corporate bonds. At its best, *best-in-class* reflects concerns that echo the Beatitudes of Jesus (Mt. 5:1-12)—hungering and thirsting for justice, contributing the hard work to make peace and grow harmony, reaching out to include the poor or marginalized, and attending with mercy to all the relationships touched or impacted by an investment. Such proactive positive investing provides the investor a unique opportunity to be faith-aligned and CST-guided with investment objectives and types. As with *impact investing*, strategies drawing on *best-in-class* will require a different level of professional expertise. These strategies should not be confused with those perfectly legitimate investments often made to support the underlying social or ecological mission of a fund or organization while protecting the invested capital and receiving a minimal or concessional rate of return. Rather, *impact investing*, and related *best-in-class* strategies expect reasonable returns consistent with the investment objectives of the investor and in line with returns from other investments.

– Using direct comparison of the competitors within their sector, the above approach makes it possible to identify the innovators and exemplars according to the stated ethical priorities. Such criteria, as examined below, comprise both enhancement and exclusion—both positive and negative evaluations.[97]

Issues to be evaluated include the quality and integrity of governance, and how human relationships are managed with their shareholders, employees, customers, suppliers, regulators, stakeholders, and even critics and competitors. Respect for dignity is basic. In addition, issuers must also be assessed by their commitment to labour and social standards (for example access to affordable housing, corporate social responsibility) and to participation schemes, such as profit sharing and employee stock ownership. In the ecological sphere, climate protection, renewable energy activities and other environmental management systems are to be used as evaluative criteria either for an efficient risk management of the investments or for the opportunities they can offer.[98]

– Enhancing obviously involves engaging—the active participation with corporations or issuers whereby investors leverage their position as shareholders to help shape policies, reforms, and decisions via dialogue with leaders and stakeholders. Asset owners must choose the priority areas consistent with their respective goals, identity and mission, searching for those projects, funds and opportunities that are aligned with their *investment policy statement*. Those seeking guidance might study alone, or with the governing group, the recent social teachings of Pope Benedict XVI (*Caritas in veritate*), and Pope Francis, (*Laudato si'* and *Fratelli tutti*). Alternatively, they might explore, in detail, the faith-and-CST-consistent parts of the United Nations Sustainable Development Goals (adopted in 2015). As always, the experience of other practitioners provides valuable reference.

The Practical Guidance from *Mensuram Bonam*

iii) ESG enhanced with CST. Investors may well benefit from the evolving ESG investing platforms which are being developed to enable companies to be evaluated and scored on their commitments and records on *environmental, social* and *governance* criteria. Many of the underlying factors for ESG resonate with the aims underlying CST, creating a potential for new synergy between value and values. The opportunity going forward, from the stance of faith-based investing, is to apply CST in two ways. First, to help heighten the quality of performance for each factor, such as enhancing the practical measures for *environmental* performance with moral terms from social justice and integral ecology; or infusing governance metrics with ethical norms for human dignity, solidarity, and the care for our common home. Second, to contribute impetus for authentic integral development by interconnecting these discrete measures systematically, such as linking *social* measures to the *environmental* outcomes exercised by *governance* by applying the ethics of the common good, or for the inclusion of the most vulnerable.

– It is crucial to note that ESG is not a synonym for CST. At its core, CST bends the trajectory of the economy and of culture to be more human and humanizing. It serves the goal of building God's Kingdom on earth. For example, the dignity of the person is a much more fulsome category than is captured in "customer satisfaction" or "employee engagement." Similarly, the dignity of duty and responsibility transcend "audit" or "privacy." Moreover, both the common good and care for our

common home, that are stipulated in CST, interpenetrate each of the ESG categories: e.g. the integral development of the person cannot be separated from her or his social milieu, nor from the natural environment that sustains life. All to say that, while ESG factors may indeed attend to parts of integral development, they neither exhaust the scope of CST, nor specifically fulfill those transcendent dimensions for recognizing the sacredness of life, the holiness and beauty of creation, and the sacramental (Eucharistic) quality of our human interconnectedness.
- Like other responsibility initiatives for markets, ESG remains a work in progress. As yet, there are no internationally ascertained and validated evaluation criteria. Beyond "greenwashing," there are examples of corporations and business associations lobbying regulators against the very social responsibility commitments that they are making to stakeholders and the public. Any ESG evaluation therefore needs to be scrutinized by the priorities and criteria for faith-coherence.[99] It should be remembered that accounting standards for finance developed over many decades, and continue to evolve. Responsibility norms such as ESG involve another level of complexity, which means that standardization will be that much more difficult. MB brings the perspective of Catholic faith to this crucial work to recall, renew, and reinforce moral aspects that are intrinsic to any economic exchange. With interest in this type of faith-based investing growing, the quantity and quality of information from which to draw meaningful comparisons among investment opportunities will also increase.
- In those regions of the world where trusted conventional financial investment opportunities are not

The Practical Guidance from *Mensuram Bonam*

as available, an institution can use CST to invest in local ventures, such as real estate development, community infrastructure, or agriculture. Where benchmarks are not developed, it can be challenging to adopt faith-consistent and socially responsible asset management. However, these obstacles can, in part, be overcome through collaboration with other groups or investors who share the commitment to CST principles.

- *Call to exclude.* The *exclusionary policy* adopts the reference values from faith, determining what may be defined as permitted, excluded or limited investment areas. Exclusionary Screening and criteria make it possible for the investor to avoid ethical contradictions between an investment and the teachings of the Church. The key is to use the "lens" from CST for prayerful assessment of the activities.

The implementation of exclusionary criteria results in the generation of a list of the companies, products, services, and funds that are to be excluded from the investable arena. In this process, investment opportunities must be evaluated against an institution's beliefs and values and the sustainability axes of ESG—ecological, social, and governance criteria. Often the criteria used will embrace some of the most pressing issues and challenges that societies and communities confront. Evaluation criteria often touch upon elementary threats to human dignity and human rights, societal coexistence, and care for creation, as well as threats to the fields of business and commercial practices in the industry being considered. Exclusionary criteria must apply based on the particular line of business of an enterprise, such as involvement in abortion or pornography, or on the basis of business practices regardless of the line of business, such as child labour or slavery.

For persons responsible for the management of the Church's assets the range of possible exclusionary criteria is considerable. The following table lists 24 categories of concern or prohibition. By no means definitive, this list identifies issues for investors which require discernment from faith, and which have already been examined by various local Episcopal Conferences.

Upholding the intrinsic dignity of human life	Avoiding destructive behaviours	Recognizing global and sustainability impacts	Securing environmental protection
Abortion	Addictive substances and services	Breaches of labour law	Threats to climate change
Armaments	Dehumanizing computer games and toys	Corruption	Exploitive negative externalities
Nuclear weapons	Pornography	Discrimination	Food availability denied for the most vulnerable
Capital Punishment		Human rights violations	Genetic engineering
Contraceptives		Rights violations of Indigenous Peoples	Hazardous chemicals
Embryo stem cell research		Totalitarian regimes	Mining and mineral commodities
Animal abuse/ experimentation		Unfair business practices	Inaccessibility to safe drinking water

(Details in the Appendix.)

There are other situations when a faith-compliance policy may prohibit the investor from associating with seemingly exemplary firms, such as those scoring high on all ESG dimensions while producing or marketing a specific product that is incompatible with the norms and values of faith. As noted, ESG is not a proxy for CST. The crux of a faith-based approach is striking the balance between prudent resource management to fund the mission of the investing entity and investing in a manner that is reflective of its Catholic identity—its faith and mission. The first responsibility should not supersede the second. In other words, some investment instruments and forms of investment, due to their inherent characteristics, are unsuitable for combining the use of capital with the promotion of the common good—even if this means that investors lose out on the benefits (for example, diversification) of such products.[100]

43. The moral imperative sometimes presents clear situations in which exclusion without exception has to be applied, such as involvement in abortion and murder. In other situations, however, there are grey areas that may require additional research, new metrics, or third-party consultation, before an informed and moral decision can be made. These include the abuse of "speculative products or investment techniques," or using accounting practice loopholes that exploit the protection of tax havens. Another complication relates to mixed investments, where an enterprise may engage in positive activities, while also directly or indirectly effecting undesirable outcomes or practices. Considering these nuances, investors may decide for faith-coherence to exclude such a company. Or they may deploy engagement to influence change while setting specific thresholds for faith-consistent performance. As with the implementation of the *best-in-class* approach, institutions must undertake this analysis internally or retain external agencies with expertise in these matters. If such resources are not available, institutions can instruct investment advisers to follow prescribed principles when selecting investments.

HABITS FOR PRACTICUM.

44. Changing the horizon or culture for investment begins by re-setting each of the steps in an investor's undertaking of due diligence.

i) **Integrate CST principles throughout the investment decision-making process.** Boards and executives will need to have faith-based or faith-consistent goals for governance and investment.

  – Allocate time and resources to develop a formal policy, and regularly monitor investments for adherence to principles of CST;
  – Stay up-to-date on the evolution and availability of investment options that reflect CST;
  – When dealing with external investment managers, assess their expertise and values for translating investment policy into faith-consistent decisions;
  – Request that principles of CST be included in new research, with evolving analysis to report on CST principle-related performance.[101]

ii) **Engage actively and positively in implementing the faith-consistent investment policy.** Risk parameters are to be revised to include ethical realities as well as economic considerations. Based on the CST principles, a new double-entry listing can be added to accounting and audit—in this case specifying the ethical assets and liabilities that paint the full picture for performance.

  – Seek out credible third-party sources, or question business enterprises at the national and international level directly regarding relevant norms, standards, and codes of conduct;
  – Pursue, where feasible, an engagement strategy grounded on principles of CST;
  – With respect to public companies, support shareholder initiatives and resolutions, promote related

The Practical Guidance from *Mensuram Bonam*

disclosure, and request standardized reporting on principles of CST;
- Exercise voting rights with respect to public companies or monitor compliance with voting policy.

iii) **Be proactive—advocating and advancing faith-consistent investing based on CST.** Enlarge norms of prudence and professionalism to include more of the ethical considerations.

- In the spirit of solidarity, encourage and help other institutions to develop and implement their FCI policy;
- Support financial actors producing investment solutions that are consistent with CST;
- Re-envision strategic allocation, and challenge the conventional ways of financial reasoning so as grow habits for faith-consideration.
- When hiring investment service providers or consultants, Catholic asset owners must evaluate both financial competence and integrity factors, such as: reputation; consistency between the corporate social responsibility claims and performance; quality of ethical governance; proven respect for regulations; and faith-alignment of proposed strategies.

iv) **Innovate, learn, and share lessons.** The mission or vocation of aligning investment with faith becomes a living process, with each stage of decision-making tuned to the outcome of integral development. Part of this mission includes continuous learning—adopting a system of analysis and training, to methodically foster the necessary skills, attitudes and values for faith-based investment.

- Seek cooperation whenever possible with ecumenical and interfaith colleagues to further the ethical investment agenda;[102]
- Foster appropriate formation of participants for a better knowledge of investment-related CST.
- Faith-consistent criteria allow investors to make concrete decisions regarding enhancement and exclusions (See 41). Appreciating the creativity of each institution and asset manager, both the exclusionary policy and the enhancing policy for positive investments to be part of the investment policy statement.
- Monitoring progress in implementing the faith-guided investment process, and monitoring results with a faith-lens, to build capacity for future investments.
- Monitor activities and progress at the governing body level and communicate those strategies and findings to institutional constituencies;
- In a manner appropriate to the governance of each institution, communicate with beneficiaries how CST is integrated into the faith-consistent policy;
- Regularly review the policy to assure relevance to current ethical considerations, the current activities and resources of the institution, and the consideration of evolving investment options that reflect the aims of the policy.

45. MB cannot at this stage address every situation nor answer every question. What is important is that MB encourages and helps Catholics and Catholic-inspired asset owners to begin or continue the journey—to integrate CST into their investment decision-making process by developing appropriate policies and practices (even if initially limited to only certain asset classes). Investing with faith is a critical and continuous process,

The Practical Guidance from *Mensuram Bonam*

which will be improved through the challenges that asset owners and managers address successfully with their gifts of faithfulness and creativity. In that spirit, this policy for good measures is not a static document, fixed and final, but rather a stimulus for the much-needed shared learning our current complexities demand. MB will be reviewed and updated regularly, to share papal or social teaching, to delve into new issues or ethical challenges, and to share lessons from investors' innovations in applying CST. Faith-consistent investment is already a growing factor in markets. For moral coherence in responding to the crises of this time, this consistency and alignment with faith is no longer an option for Catholic investors and asset owners.

46. Advocating a change in values as well as priorities, MB adds another element to the Catholic Church's contributions for more human management practices in all sectors of the economy. In keeping with her mission, the Church will also continue to reinforce the ethical and anthropological footing of the financial system. As it has in all her social teachings, the Church will be steadfast in redirecting economic activities to promote the dignity and integral development of every human being and the care of our common home. In that context, MB presents an avenue whereby the Church can practically and positively continue to engage the principles and operations of the financial system and ensure that they are at the service of the common good. MB calls for a dialogue with financiers, politicians and International Organizations, such as the UN, which share a keen interest in these issues. And to make progress together on this journey, MB offers a vision for how the aims of ethical or socially responsible investing can evolve to fuller fruitfulness in light of Catholic Social Teaching.

CONCLUSION

SHARING THE WORK.

47. As a call to action, MB looks forward—to the innovations and lessons from Catholic investors as they continue in their efforts to tangibly contribute to integral human development. New metrics are definitely needed to quantify outcomes for responsibility. That said, faith is a belief that is held fast before answers or data provide corroboration. In the current reality of markets and investments, often absent are the humanizing qualities of deeper purpose and historical perspective. Faith's wisdom is key, not because it has engineered precise answers, but for exposing the moral possibilities from our relationship with God-who-loves. When things seem improbable if not impossible, we can recall that the general teachings about the Kingdom of God in the Scriptures unfold under a tension between the here-and-now and the not-yet; between the present and the future. God is always at the center. God is always near.[103]

48. As much as this document draws upon CST, and as urgent as are the details for faith-consistent implementation, MB invites all investors to prayerful discernment while analyzing options and making decisions. Part of this reflective approach entails resting from work, as God modelled after the six days of creation (Gen. 2:1-3), as well as relishing the holiness of the Sabbath, which God set as a commandment for liberation and re-creation (Ex. 20:8-11). Markets are forever frenetic and so can be all-consuming of attention. However, as Pope Francis emphasizes in his writings and teachings, the very crises that require

our efforts and conscientiousness compel us to dream—to look beyond the exigencies of the moment so as to imagine what is needed, and possible, for progress on integral human development.[104] Each investor will have their own aims, and will bring to bear in their own way their faith-commitments to their decisions and practices. The call to dream is to help "the human heart to be open with trust to the God who not only has created all that exists, but has also given us himself in Jesus Christ. The Lord, who is the first to care for us, teaches us to care for our brothers and sisters and the environment."[105]

> "You are young people from 115 countries. I ask you to recognize our need for one another in giving birth to an economic culture able to plant dreams, draw forth prophecies and visions, allow hope to flourish, inspire trust, bind up wounds, weave together relationships, awaken a dawn of hope, learn from one another and create a bright resourcefulness that will enlighten minds, warm hearts, give strength to our hands, and inspire in young people—all young people, with no one excluded—a vision of the future filled with the joy of the Gospel."
>
> Pope Francis—Video Message to Participants of "The Economy of Francesco"
> 21 November 2020

49. To reiterate the key objectives outlined in the introduction, MB calls for the urgent implementation and development of investment measures predicated by consistency with faith. A starting point and call-to-action, MB offers moral guidance from faith and CST to help investors and institutions continue in practical and concrete terms to look beyond ordinary goals and contribute to the well-being of all. Integrating the Church's social

Conclusion

and moral teaching into the management of financial assets is crucial for both personal moral coherence and to contribute positively to needed changes in the economy and society. Even more specific and detailed policies have been issued by local and magisterial teaching bodies, which MB cherishes and seeks to complement.

50. Indeed, the commitment to greater alignment between the management of assets and the broader mission of the Church should be further enhanced through cooperation between Catholic asset owners at a national and international level—including Vatican and Holy See entities. Sharing resources and strategies, promoting joint action to engage more effectively and efficiently with particular companies, and coordinating advocacy approaches towards policy makers at various levels of government are all steps to be encouraged. With such a 'network' of specialists, CST will become a reliable and effective reference for the overall financial services sector. Influencing the influential areas of finance in this way opens new horizons for evangelization. Helping to open or grow responsible channels for communication between all investors of good will, this greater cooperation will produce synergy and accelerate the scaling-up of similar responsibility initiatives. MB sets the new normal for Catholic investors. It is also an example of lessons from the social experience and teachings of the Church that may be of guidance to the economy and culture at large.

ONLY A BEGINNING. WHAT'S NEXT?

51. In Luke's Gospel, Christ's promise of a good measure is from our participating in relationship with God, and including others in those loving benefits. God's math for abundance is not ours—or at least not yet ours. Nevertheless, every time we recite the Our Father we invoke the good measure of God's

plentitude, as both a hopeful mystery, and a transforming promise from being in relationship to one another as well as with God.

It is important for all of us, especially investors, to live in this nexus of relationships—to act, talk and meet on a regular basis to monitor, review, and propose adjustments to the shared project (and shared responsibility) for integral development in all its forms. Sharing in such dialogue is critical considering, in particular, the permanent process of innovation that is taking place in the financial sector. Neither the first nor the last word on faith-consistent investing, MB will continue to contribute to the flow of good measures. Lessons from Bishop's conferences and investor best practices will be shared on an on-going basis, including with specific questions and innovations from the Church's living tradition of faith. Studies and workshops on implementing investing-with-CST will be undertaken, again with the aim of disseminating new and more precise guidance. As well as collaborating with other sciences and disciplines to forge new ethical metrics, MB will continue to provide good measures in the sense of recommended processes and tools for moral investigation and integration. "Old models are disappearing," observes Pope Benedict XVI, "but promising new ones are taking shape on the horizon."[106] It is towards that horizon that all of us are called to journey, living our faith by integrally investing our gifts and talents as well as our assets.

APPENDIX— EXCLUSIONARY CRITERIA

1. Intrinsic dignity of human life	Issue in Brief
Abortion	• The taking of human life, even at its earliest stage when an egg cell and sperm cell join, is unambiguously condemned by the Church as an abusive expression of human dominion over life and death. (*Compendium*, n. 233).
Armaments	• Military conflicts always cost human lives. The uncontrolled proliferation of arms facilitates many outbreaks of violence and erodes secure peace. Thus, industries which thrive on the production of these instruments of war and destruction engage in a reprehensible business.
Nuclear Weapons	• The Church's teaching, as reiterated by Pope Francis, is that "the use of nuclear weapons, as well as their mere possession, is immoral." The premise of nuclear weapons as deterrence is flawed, as it "inevitably ends up poisoning relationships between peoples and obstructing any possible form of real dialogue" (Message to the *First Meeting of States Parties to the Treaty on the Prohibition of Nuclear Weapons* (TPNW), 21 June 2022).
Capital Punishment	• Countries that apply the death penalty place themselves above the fundamental right to life. The punishment of offenders, the protection of society and the deterrence of other potential offenders can be achieved through other means.

Continued

Contraceptives	• Maintaining both the unitive (common life project) and procreative significances of human sexuality within marriage defends against slipping into a merely recreational approach to sexuality that generates egoism and often leads to further abuse (*Compendium* n. 233 and Saint Paul VI, *Humanae Vitae*, 11).
Embryo Stem Cell Research	• The priority attached to conserving human life prohibits using embryo stem cells for research purposes. Economic interests, that may lead to the industrial exploitation and use of people, are always to be subordinated to the right to life.
Animal Experimentation	• As part of Creation, animals are subject to a duty of care and stewardship by those whom God has created in his own image. Animal experimentation that goes beyond the requirements of medical science, for instance in the cosmetic industry, is difficult to reconcile with the conservation of non-human Creation.
2. Patterns leading to addiction and abuse	**Issue in Brief**
Addictive Substances or Services	• Addictive substances such as tobacco, alcohol, and drugs, and certain services, such as gambling, can harm people. Addiction is a disease that seriously damages health, destroys life and carries high social costs.
Computer Games/Toys	• Computer games or toys that glorify violence are not only potentially addictive. They can make players, especially young children, more aggressive, dull their sensitivities towards violence, and blur the boundaries between the virtual and real world.
Pornography	• Pornography breaches personal dignity, rendering the person acting a mere object, while deforming the person watching. Pornography constitutes moral misconduct.
3. Global impacts and sustainable development	**Issue in Brief**
Breaches of Labour Law	• The Church explicitly demands the right to decent work as the milieu in which the human personality can grow and thrive. Exploitative child labour, forced labour, human trafficking, restriction of freedom of assembly and discrimination based on gender, race, origin, religion, or political views are to be decisively countered.

Continued

Appendix—Exclusionary Criteria

Corruption	• The greatest impediments to sustainable development are bribery and corruption. Phenomena present in all fields, bribery and corruption exacerbate inequalities, distort justice, and abuse the common good to enrich a few at the expense of the many.
Discrimination	• As stated in *The Catechism*: "Every form of social or cultural discrimination in fundamental personal rights on the grounds of sex, race, colour, social conditions, language, or religion must be curbed and eradicated as incompatible with God's design" (*Catechism*, 1935).
Human Rights Violations	• The Church recognizes the human rights of all people, without distinction on any grounds. These rights need to be promoted and defended with unceasing commitment. Human rights violations destroy both dignity and opportunities for development.
The Overlooked Rights of Indigenous Peoples	• Often unseen for being at the margins, the rights of indigenous peoples must be aggressively and appropriately protected, including their relationship to their lands, culture, arts and resources.
Totalitarian Violence and Oppression	• Totalitarian regimes or military dictatorships exercise power through dehumanizing fear. Neither human life nor civil society can develop fully when powers sequester themselves in privilege while abusing the rights of citizens.
Unfair/Unethical Business Practices	• Cartel formation, price agreements, insider trading, false accounting, money laundering, bribery, human trafficking, lack of transparency, and tax evasion are among the business practices that cheat society and undermine the efficiency of markets.
4. Environmental protection	**Issue in Brief**
Climate Change	• "Civilization requires energy, but energy use must not destroy civilization…There is an urgent need to develop policies so that, in the next few years, the emission of carbon dioxide and other highly polluting gases can be drastically reduced, for example, substituting for fossil fuels and developing sources of renewable energy" (Pope Francis, addressing *The Energy Transition and Care for our Common Home*, Vatican City, 14 June 2019).

Continued

Exploitation of the Environment	The Christian mission is to cherish and conserve Creation as God's gift. CST condemns disrespect for ecological standards, particularly as the costs for consumption and pollution often fall to the vulnerable who had little or no role in unsustainable practices.
Food and Agricultural Commodities	• The right to food, like the right to water, is rooted in the dignity of the human person. Its availability and supply are an ethical imperative that overrides purely economic rationale and makes commodity speculation untenable. While the science of food production is encouraged, it should not privilege the powerful in land distribution and use.
Green/Genetic Engineering	• Potential for ethical conflict exists on at least several levels: the environmental and health risks not yet precisely defined from new technology; its relationship with traditional plant breeding; and the consequences for food security—especially in developing countries where multinational groups patent seeds to dominate the market.
Hazardous Chemicals and Climate-Damaging Substances	• Hazardous chemicals constitute a threat to humanity and to the environment. Toxic waste and eco-system contamination besmirch Creation, undermine human health, and leave residues that will have untold consequences for future generations.
Mining and Minerals Commodities	• Mineral commodities are indispensable for the modern economy. However, extraction may entail exploitative environmental conduct or breaches of fundamental labour rights, particularly in developing countries where mining is often at the heart of conflict.
Clean Water	• "The right to water, as all human rights, finds its basis in human dignity and not in any kind of merely quantitative assessment that considers water as a merely economic good. Without water, life is threatened. Therefore, the right to safe drinking water is a universal and inalienable right" (*Compendium*, n. 485).

NOTES

1. *Pastoral Constitution on the Church in the Modern World* (*Gaudium et spes*), 7 December 1965, 3, https://www.vatican.va/archive/hist_councils/ii_vatican_council/documents/vat-ii_const_19651207_gaudium-et-spes_en.html.
2. "Finance is an important sector of the economy which embraces several activities including investing. However, as an activity, finance must actively be at the service of the real economy and not be used solely as a means of unproductive speculation."
3. *Caritas in veritate*, 9.
4. *Caritas in veritate*, 9.
5. *Caritas in veritate*, 9.
6. *Gaudium et spes*, 91.
7. Elena Beccalli, Paolo Camoletto, John Dalla Costa, Jean-Baptiste Douville de Franssu, Rev. Séamus Finn, Robert G. Kennedy, Mark Krcmaric, Pierre de Lauzun, Rev. Thomas McClain, Rev. Nicola Riccardi, Antoine de Salins, Anna Maria Tarantola, Alessandra Viscovi, Helge Wulsdorf, and Stefano Zamagni.
8. ECHo Fund, consultancy group, 55 Silwood Road, Bramley, Johannesburg, with representatives in East Africa (Kenya), West Africa (Ghana), and Central Africa (DR Congo), assisting local churches with financing church missions.
9. Francis, *Evangelii gaudium*, apostolic exhortation, Vatican City, 3 November 2013, 57, https://www.vatican.va/content/francesco/en/apost_exhortations.index.html, accessed 21 July 2022.

10. Benedict XVI, *Caritas in veritate*, encyclical, Vatican City, 29 June 2009, 45–46, https://www.vatican.va/content/benedict-xvi/en/encyclicals/documents/hf_ben-xvi_enc_20090629_caritas-in-veritate.html, accessed 21 July 2022.

11. Paul VI, *Populorum progressio*, encyclical, 26 March 1967, 20, https://www.vatican.va/content/paul-vi/en/encyclicals/documents/hf_p-vi_enc_26031967_populorum.html, accessed 21 July 2022.

12. UN Secretary-General Ban Ki-Moon, statement at the presentation of the Sustainable Development Goals framework, UN General Assembly, 2015.

13. *Dogmatic Constitution on the Church (Lumen gentium)*, 21 November 1964, chap. 4, sec. 33, https://www.vatican.va/archive/hist_councils/ii_vatican_council/documents/vat-ii_const_19641121_lumen-gentium_en.html, accessed 16 September 2022.

14. *Caritas in veritate*, 41, 71.

15. Dicastery for Promoting Integral Human Development, *Vocation of the Business Leader: A Reflection*, 5th ed., 2018; and 8th International Conference on Catholic Social Thought and Management Education, "Renewing Mission and Identity in Catholic Business Education," University of Dayton, 18–20 June 2012.

16. "Banking on the Common Good, Finance for the Common Good," seminar paper, San Calisto, 13 May 2013; and Peter Turkson, "The Future of the Corporation: From Best in the World to Best for the World," University of the Andes, Chile, 2016; cf. Michael Sean Winters, "Cardinal Turkson: Business Vocation," *National Catholic Reporter*, https://www.ncronline.org/blog/distinctly-catholic/cardinal-turkson-business-vocation.

17. Holy See Press Office, Bulletin no. 075, 22 September 2022, "Audience to Participants at the Deloitte Global Meeting."

Notes

18. Francis, *Laudato si'*, encyclical, 24 May 2015, 13, https://www.vatican.va/content/francesco/en/encyclicals/documents/papa-francesco_20150524_enciclica-laudato-si.html, accessed 16 July 2022.

19. Austrian Bishops' Conference, *Ethical Investment Guidelines* (Katholische Kirche Österreich), *Amtsblatt der Österreichischen Bischofskonferenz*, no. 74, 1 January 2018.

20. United States Conference of Catholic Bishops, *Economic Justice for All: Pastoral Letter on Catholic Social Teaching and the U.S. Economy*, 1986, 6.

21. Italian Bishops' Conference, *La Chiesa Cattolica e la gestione delle risorse finanziarie con criteri etici di responsabilità sociale, ambientale e di governance*, Documentazione CEI, 9 March 2020, 3, https://economato.chiesacattolica.it/linee-guida-per-gli-investimenti-sostenibili-ed-etici/.

22. *Mensuram bonam*, chap. 2.

23. *Caritas in veritate*, 71.

24. Francis (with Austen Ivereigh), *Let Us Dream: The Path to a Better Future*, Kindle ed. (New York: Simon & Schuster, 2020), 4–6.

25. *Catechism of the Catholic Church*, 14.

26. *Catechism of the Catholic Church*, 25.

27. *Caritas in veritate*, 42.

28. *Caritas in veritate*, 51.

29. *Laudato si'*, 239.

30. *Laudato si'*, 239.

31. *Laudato si'*, 240.

32. Francis, General Audience, 27 January 2021, https://www.vatican.va/content/francesco/en/audiences/2021/documents/papa-francesco_20210127_udienza-generale.html, accessed 26 July 2022.

33. Francis, General Audience, 27 January 2021.

34. *Populorum progressio*, 32.
35. *Caritas in veritate*, 7.
36. Cf. *Journal of Catholic Social Thought* 10, no. 2 (2013).
37. John Paul II, homily, 27 October 1991, on Adolf Kolping; cf. *Laudato si'*, 231.
38. Pontifical Council for Justice and Peace, *Compendium of the Social Doctrine of the Church* (Vatican City: Libreria Editrice Vaticana, 2004).
39. Cf. Benedict XVI, *Caritas in veritate*, 2009; Francis, *Evangelii gaudium*, 2013; *Laudato si'*, 2015; *Fratelli tutti*, 2020.
40. Francis and Ahmad Al-Tayyeb, *Human Fraternity for World Peace and Living Together* (Vatican City: Libreria Editrice Vaticana, 2019).
41. Cf. John Paul II, *Fides et ratio*; *Veritatis splendor*.
42. *Gaudium et spes*, 56.
43. *Caritas in veritate*, 56.
44. *Compendium of the Social Doctrine of the Church*, 161.
45. Definition of "human dignity" as comprising the dignity of each human being, of each human community, and dignity in human rights.
46. The Greek *adelphos/adelphē* (brother/sister) means "from the same womb." Cf. *Fratelli tutti*, 22, 98.
47. Cf. purpose of the UN Sustainable Development Goals (SDGs) as formulated by Ban Ki-Moon, UN General Assembly, 2015.
48. Amartya Sen, *Development as Freedom* (Oxford: Oxford University Press, 2001), 291; cf. Martha C. Nussbaum, *Creating Capabilities: The Human Development Approach* (Cambridge, MA: Harvard University Press, 2011), 21–22.
49. Cf. *Catechism of the Catholic Church*, 357, 11 April 2003, https://www.vatican.va/archive/ENG0015/_INDEX.HTM.
50. *Caritas in veritate*, 18.
51. *Caritas in veritate*, 1; cf. Eph. 1:4-5.

Notes

52. Francis, Address to Moneyval, 8 October 2020, https://www.vatican.va/content/francesco/en/speeches/2020/october/documents/papa-francesco_20201008_comitato-moneyval.html; cf. *Evangelii gaudium*, 58.

53. *Compendium of the Social Doctrine of the Church*, 164.

54. *Compendium of the Social Doctrine of the Church*, 164.

55. *Laudato si'*, 156.

56. *Compendium of the Social Doctrine of the Church*, 61.

57. Definition of "common good" from Aristotelian philosophy; cf. Aristotle, *Nicomachean Ethics* V.2 (1130b 25); VIII.14 (1163b 5–15); John XXIII, *Mater et magistra*, 48, 65; *Pacem in terris*, 58.

58. John XXIII, *Mater et magistra*, encyclical, 15 May 1961, 48, 136, https://www.vatican.va/content/john-xxiii/en/encyclicals/documents/hf_j-xxiii_enc_15051961_mater.html, accessed 14 September 2022.

59. *Mater et magistra*, 65; cf. John XXIII, *Pacem in terris*, encyclical, 11 April 1963, 58, https://www.vatican.va/content/john-xxiii/en/encyclicals/documents/hf_j-xxiii_enc_11041963_pacem.html, accessed 14 September 2022.

60. Francis, *Fratelli tutti*, 3 October 2020, 108, https://www.vatican.va/content/francesco/en/encyclicals/documents/papa-francesco_20201003_enciclica-fratelli-tutti.html, accessed 8 August 2022.

61. *Fratelli tutti*, 182.

62. "Moneyval," Council of Europe, https://www.coe.int/en/web/moneyval, accessed 7 November 2020.

63. Cf. Francis, Address to Moneyval, 8 October 2020.

64. Francis, *Fratelli tutti*, 94, 99, 106, 142, 183.

65. *Laudato si'*, 58.

66. John Paul II, *Sollicitudo rei socialis*, encyclical, 30 December 1987, 38, https://www.vatican.va/content/john-paul-ii/en/encyclicals/documents/hf_jp-ii_enc_30121987_sollicitudo-rei-socialis.html, accessed 21 July 2022.

67. Pontifical Council for Justice and Peace, *Work as Key to the Social Question: The Great Social and Economic Transformations and the Subjective Dimension of Work* (Vatican City: Libreria Editrice Vaticana, 2002), 356.

68. Cf. *Compendium of the Social Doctrine of the Church*, 201–3.

69. Benedict XVI, *Caritas in veritate*, 35–36; cf. Francis, *Fratelli tutti*, 22; United Nations, "World Day of Social Justice," https://www.un.org/en/observances/social-justice-day.

70. Cf. *Compendium of the Social Doctrine of the Church*, 187.

71. Cf. *Compendium of the Social Doctrine of the Church*, 186–89; *Vocation of the Business Leader*, 51–52.

72. Benedict XVI, Message for the World Day of Peace, 2010, "If You Want to Cultivate Peace, Protect Creation," https://www.vatican.va/content/benedict-xvi/en/messages/peace/documents/hf_ben-xvi_mes_20091208_xliii-world-day-peace.html.

73. Francis of Assisi, "Canticle of the Creatures."

74. *Evangelii gaudium*, 186.

75. *Evangelii gaudium*, 198.

76. *Caritas in veritate*, 19.

77. *Caritas in veritate*, 51.

78. *Laudato si'*, 70.

79. *Laudato si'*, 141.

80. *Laudato si'*, 120, 138; cf. *Vocation of the Business Leader*, 55.

81. *Caritas in veritate*, 14, 22, 52.

82. *Gaudium et spes*, 9.

83. *Gaudium et spes*, 9; *Laudato si'*, 141.

84. "Global Impact Investing Network," https://www.thegiin.org, accessed 7 November 2020.

Notes

85. Francis, "A Big Heart Open to God," *America*, 19 September 2013, https://www.americamagazine.org/faith/2013/09/30/big-heart-open-god-interview-pope-francis.
86. *Laudato si'*, 194.
87. "Faith Plans," https://www.faithplans.org; FaithInvest, https://www.faithinvest.org/_files/ugd/72b7c5_8f781c73c1bc4691a18cb9b3ace4e53b.pdf.
88. *Let Us Dream*, 5–6.
89. *Let Us Dream*, 54–61, 145–46.
90. Franciscan initiative of the *Monti di Pietà*, begun Perugia 1462; cf. modern microcredit and ethical finance.
91. Definition of ETF (Exchange-Traded Fund).
92. Definition of EU SFDR Regulation (Sustainable Finance Disclosure Regulation).
93. Morningstar Manager Research, "Sustainable Investing Research Suggests No Performance Penalty," https://www.morningstar.com/articles/779758/sustainable-investing-research-suggests-no-performance-penalty.
94. "World's Most Ethical Companies: Five-Year Ethics Premium 24%," 2022, https://worldsmostethicalcompanies.com, accessed 12 September 2022.
95. *Caritas in veritate*, 40, 45.
96. *Laudato si'*, 10, 11, 62.
97. Deutsche Bischofskonferenz/Zentralkomitee der deutschen Katholiken, *Making Ethically Sustainable Investments*, n. 25, https://www.nachhaltig-predigen.de/dokumente/cmsj/.
98. *Making Ethically Sustainable Investments*, n. 25.
99. United States Conference of Catholic Bishops, *Socially Responsible Investment Guidelines*, November 2021, https://www.usccb.org/resources/Socially%20Responsible%20Investment%20Guidelines%202021%20(003).pdf.
100. Austrian Bishops' Conference, *Amtsblatt*, no. 74, p. 15.

101. "Investment," Wikipedia, https://en.wikipedia.org/wiki/Investment.

102. *The Zug Guidelines to Faith-Consistent Investing*, Faith in Finance, ARC, 2017, http://www.arcworld.org/downloads/ZUG_Guidelines_to_FCI_2017.pdf.

103. "Economy of Francesco Covenant," Vatican News, September 2022, https://www.vaticannews.va/en/pope/news/2022-09/economy-francesco-final-covenant-pope-francis-gospel.html.

104. Francis, *Querida Amazonia*, apostolic exhortation, 2 February 2020, 8, 28, 41, 61, https://www.vatican.va/content/francesco/en/apost_exhortations/documents/papa-francesco_esortazione-ap_20200202_querida-amazonia.html, accessed 17 September 2022.

105. *Querida Amazonia*, 41.

106. *Caritas in veritate*, 40.

SELECTED BIBLIOGRAPHY

Key sources in the Scriptures

Genesis 2:15, 1:26-27—on care for the common home

Matthew 5:3-12 Beatitudes; 7:17-19; 13 "Parables of the Kingdom": Parable of the Hidden Treasure (13: 44); Parable of the Pearl of Great Price (13:45-46); Parable of the Tenant Farmer (21:33-45); Parable of the Talents (25:14-30)

Mark 4:26-29

Luke 5:1-11 Miraculous catch of fish; 6:20-31, 6:32-36, 6:38; 16:1-13; 19-31 The Rich Man and Lazarus; 7:21, 24-27; 13: 24-30; 25:1-13; 25:14-30

James 2:14-17

Revelation 21:5

Letter of Saint Paul to the Galatians 5:6

Second Letter of Saint Paul to the Corinthians 5:17

Papal Magisterium

Saint John XXIII, Encyclical Letter *Mater et magistra* on Christianity and social progress, 1961. https://www.vatican.va/content/john-xxiii/en/encyclicals/documents/hf_j-xxiii_enc_15051961_mater.html.

Saint John XXIII, Encyclical Letter *Pacem in terris* on establishing universal peace in truth, justice, charity and liberty, 1963. https://www.vatican.va/content/john-xxiii/en/encyclicals/documents/hf_j-xxiii_enc_11041963_pacem.html.

Saint Paul VI, *Gaudium et spes*, Pastoral Constitution on the Church and the Modern World, 1965. https://www.vatican.va/archive/hist_councils/ii_vatican_council/documents/vat-ii_const_19651207_gaudium-et-spes_en.html.

Vatican Council II, Decree on the Apostolate of the Laity *Apostolicam Actuositatem*, promulgated by His Holiness Pope Paul VI, 1965. https://www.vatican.va/archive/hist_councils/ii_vatican_council/documents/vat-ii_decree_19651118_apostolicam-actuositatem_en.html.

Saint Paul VI, Encyclical Letter *Populorum progressio* on the development of peoples, 1967. https://www.vatican.va/content/paul-vi/en/encyclicals/documents/hf_p-vi_enc_26031967_populorum.html.

Saint Paul VI, Encyclical Letter *Humanae Vitae* on the regulation of birth, 1968. https://www.vatican.va/content/paul-vi/en/encyclicals/documents/hf_p-vi_enc_25071968_humanae-vitae.html.

Saint John Paul II, Encyclical Letter *Laborem exercens* on human work on the ninetieth anniversary of *Rerum Novarum*, 1981. https://www.vatican.va/content/john-paul-ii/en/encyclicals/documents/hf_jp-ii_enc_14091981_laborem-exercens.html.

Saint John Paul II, Encyclical Letter *Sollicitudo rei socialis*, for the twentieth anniversary of *Populorum progressio*, 1987. https://www.vatican.va/content/john-paul-ii/en/encyclicals/documents/hf_jp-ii_enc_30121987_sollicitudo-rei-socialis.html.

Saint John Paul II, Apostolic Constitution *Fidei depositum* on the publication of the Catechism of the Catholic Church prepared following the Second Vatican Council. https://www.vatican.va/content/john-paul-ii/en/apost_constitutions/documents/hf_jp-ii_apc_19921011_fidei-depositum.html.

Pope Benedict XVI, Encyclical Letter *Caritas in veritate* on integral human development in charity and truth, 2009. https://www.vatican.va/content/benedict-xvi/en/encyclicals/

documents/hf_ben-xvi_enc_20090629_caritas-in-veritate.html.

Pope Francis, Apostolic Exhortation *Evangelii gaudium*, 2013. https://www.vatican.va/content/francesco/en/apost_exhortations/documents/papa-francesco_esortazione-ap_20131124_evangelii-gaudium.html.

Pope Francis, Encyclical Letter *Laudato si'* on care for our common home, 2015. https://www.vatican.va/content/francesco/en/encyclicals/documents/papa-francesco_20150524_enciclica-laudato-si.html.

Pope Francis, Encyclical Letter *Fratelli tutti* on fraternity and social friendship, 2020. https://www.vatican.va/content/francesco/en/encyclicals/documents/papa-francesco_20201003_enciclica-fratelli-tutti.html.

Other Papal Messages and Discourses

Pope Francis, *Message to the Executive Chairman of the World Economic Forum on the occasion of the Annual Meeting at Davos-Klosters, Switzerland.* https://www.vatican.va/content/francesco/en/messages/pont-messages/2014/documents/papa-francesco_20140117_messaggio-wef-davos.html.

Pope Francis, *Address to Participants in the Meeting organised by the Dicastery for Promoting Integral Human Development on "The Energy Transition and Care for our Common Home,"* 2019. https://www.vatican.va/content/francesco/en/speeches/2019/june/documents/papa-francesco_20190614_compagnie-petrolifere.html.

Pope Francis, *Address to the Committee of Experts from the European Council (Moneyval)*, 8 October 2020. https://www.vatican.va/content/francesco/en/speeches/2020/october/documents/papa-francesco_20201008_comitato-moneyval.html.

Pope Francis, Video Message to the Participants in "The Economy of Francesco-young people, a Commitment, the Future," 21 November 2020. https://www.vatican.va/content/francesco/en/messages/pont-messages/2020/documents/papa-francesco_20201121_videomessaggio-economy-of-francesco.html.

Pope Francis (in conversation with Austen Ivereigh), *Let Us Dream: A Path to a Better Future*. New York, Simon & Schuster, 2020.

Publications of the Dicastery for Promoting Integral Human Development

Pontifical Council for Justice and Peace, *Work as key to the Social Question: The great social and economic transformation and the subjective dimension of work*, 2002.

Pontifical Council for Justice and Peace, Compendium of the Social Doctrine of the Church, Libreria Editrice Vaticana, 2004. https://www.vatican.va/roman_curia/pontifical_councils/justpeace/documents/rc_pc_justpeace_doc_20060526_compendio-dott-soc_en.html.

Pontifical Council for Justice and Peace, "Towards a Reform of the International Financial and Monetary Systems in the light of a global public authority," 2011. http://vatican.va/roman_curia/pontifical_councils/justpeace/documents/rc_pc_justpeace_doc_20111024_nota_en_html (06/02/2021).

Pontifical Council for Justice and Peace, "Banking on the common good, finance for the common good," Seminar Paper, San Calisto, 13 May 2013. http://www.iustitiaetpax.va/content/dam/giustiziaepace/Eventi/DOCS/BCG/2013_BANKING_LG_ENG.pdf.

Dicastery for Promoting Integral Human Development, Vocation of the Business Leader: A Reflection, Fourth edition, 2014.

Selected Bibliography

https://www.humandevelopment.va/content/dam/svil uppoumano/pubblicazioni-documenti/archivio/economia-e-finanza/vocation-of-business-leader/Vocation_ENGLISH_4th%20edition.pdf.

Cardinal Peter K.A. Turkson, Pope Francis Questions the Economy, Opening Address at the International Conference "The Economy according to Pope Francis—a case study of social market economy," Pontifical University of the Holy Cross, 13 September 2016. http://www.justpax.va/content/dam/giustiziaepace/presidenteinterventi/2016/President_Pope%20Francis%20questions%20the%20Economy_130916.pdf.

Cardinal Peter K.A. Turkson, "The Future of the Corporation: From Best in the World to Best for the World," University of the Andes, Chile, 2016.

Congregation for the Doctrine of the Faith / Dicastery for Promoting Integral Human Development, *Oeconomicae et Pecuniariae Questiones, Considerations for an Ethical Discernment Regarding Some Aspects of the Present Economic-Financial System*, 2018. https://www.vatican.va/roman_curia/congregations/cfaith/documents/rc_con_cfaith_doc_20180106_oeconomicae-et-pecuniariae_en.html.

Catholic Relief Services and the Dicastery for Promoting Integral Human Development, Vatican-CRS Seminars, 18-21 July 2018. https://viiconference.org.

Other Sources

Catechism of the Catholic Church, https://www.vatican.va/archive/ENG0015/_INDEX.HTM.

United States Conference of Catholic Bishops, *Economic Justice for All: Pastoral letter on Catholic Social Teaching and the U.S. Economy*, 1986. https://www.usccb.org/upload/economic_justice_for_all.pdf.

Conferenza Episcopale Italiana (CEI) *La Chiesa Cattolica e la gestione delle risorse finanziarie con criteri etici di responsabilità sociale, ambientale e di governance*, Documentation of the Conferenza Episcopale Italiana, 9 March 2020. https://economato.chiesacattolica.it/linee-guida-per-gli-investimenti-sostenibili-ed-etici/.

Conférence des évêques de France, Vade mecum No.3-2015, "Repères éthiques de gestion financière des biens d'Eglise, 2007. https://eglise.catholique.fr/sengager-dans-la-societe/economie/observatoire-fonds-ethiques/459480-reperes-ethiques-de-leglise-catholique-prise-compte-de-doctrine-sociale-de-leglise/.

Deutsche Bischofskonferenz / Zentralkomitee der deutschen Katholiken, *Ethisch-nachhaltig investieren Eine Orientierungshilfe für Finanzverantwortliche katholischer Einrichtungen in Deutschland*, 2. aktualisierte Auflage, 13 July 2021.

– EN: *Making Ethically Sustainable Investments 1st edition*. http://www.nachhaltig-predigen.de/dokumente/cmsj/Strukturen/Geldanlage/DBK-ZdK-Guideline EthicallyInvestment.pdf.

Global Impact Investing Network, see https://www.thegiin.org (7 November 2020).

– Impact Management Project https://impactmanagement project.com.

Intergovernmental Panel on Climate Change, Assessment Report 5 (AR5) on Mitigation of Climate Change, 2014. https://www.ipcc.ch/report/ar5/wg3/.

Österreichische Bischofskonferenz, Financial investments as cooperation: Ethical investment guidelines of the Austrian Bishops' Conference and the Religious Orders of Austria (FinAnKo) (Katholische Kirche Österreich 2018), Amtsblatt der Österreichischen Bischofskonferenz Nr. 72 (01.01.2018).

Selected Bibliography

https://www.bischofskonferenz.at/dl/mOLLJKJKkolmlJqx4kJK/Englisch_final_pdf.

United States Conference of Catholic Bishops, Socially Responsible Investment Guidelines 12.11.2003. http://www.usccb.org/about/financial-reporting/socially-responsible-investment-guidelines.cfm.

The Zug Guidelines to Faith-Consistent Investing, Faith in Finance, ARC, 2017. http://www.arcworld.org/downloads/ZUG_Guidelines_to_FCI_2017.pdf.